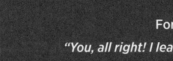

For my Dad:

"You, all right! I learned it by watching you!"

PULUTAN!

Filipino Bar Bites, Appetizers and Street Eats

MARVIN GAPULTOS

Photographs by the author

TUTTLE Publishing

Tokyo | Rutland, Vermont | Singapore

CONTENTS

WHAT IS PULUTAN?

Derived from the Filipino word *pulot*, meaning "to pick up with the fingers," *pulutan* (pronounced poo-loo-tawn) generally refers to the finger foods, appetizers, bar snacks and street foods that are best enjoyed alongside an alcoholic drink.

Historically speaking, the earliest known reference to pulutan was recorded in 1613 in the very first dictionary of the Tagalog language, *Vocabulario de la Lengua Tagala*. Within this dictionary, written by the Spanish, the entry for "*polotan*" was defined as "a type of snack which one eats while drinking wine." Considering that royal Filipino *datus* (chiefs) enjoyed the likes of turtle eggs and salted pork with their alcohol, and that indigenous Filipino wines like *pangasi* and *tapuy* (made from rice), *tuba* (made from palm sap), *lambanog* (made from coconut sap) and *basi* (made from sugarcane) existed long before colonial times, I think it's safe to say that the Spanish were not witnessing anything new with Filipinos.

Today, the spirit (no pun intended) of pulutan remains the same as in precolonial times, but with modern beer and liquor taking their place alongside traditional indigenous wines. Filipino writer Edilberto "Eddy" Alegre wrote the following about pulutan in the Philippines:

The choice of drink at most local drinking places is rather limited: beer, gin, rum, whiskey, tuba, lambanog, basi. But the choice of pulutan is limitless: legumes, vegetables, birds, pork, beef, chicken, venison, dog meat, goat, eggs, frogs, iguana, crocodile, fish, squid, octopus, shellfish. Cross that with the various ways of cooking them, and one can only marvel at how democratic and adventurous Filipino taste buds are.

Democratic and adventurous, indeed.

With a rich culinary history of worldly influences from the likes of the aforementioned Spain, along with China, the US, and more, modern pulutan can range from tapas and *pintxos* to spring rolls and dumplings, and even barbecue and hot wings. Add to that the astonishing number of indigenous Filipino creations, including everything from battered quail eggs to pigs' ears and tofu to caramelized banana skewers, and we have a very extensive and uniquely Filipino menu of food to be enjoyed with our favorite alcoholic beverages.

PULUTAN FOR THE PEOPLE

As per the tradition in the Philippines, pulutan is never eaten in solitude, but always shared among a group of hungry and thirsty family and friends. Beyond food and drink, pulutan constitutes a practice in camaraderie and social bonding.

What's more, that social bonding isn't tied to any specific time. In the West, "going out for drinks" usually means meeting your friends at a bar after work. Not so in the Philippines. Whether it's fishermen returning from the sea in the wee hours of the morning, farmers retiring in the early afternoon, business people clocking out in the early evening, or university students out on the town late at night, drinking "after hours" in the Philippines doesn't always translate to post-5 p.m. activities. And since pulutan can be served everywhere from restaurants, to bars, roadside food stalls, or in the home, they aren't tied to any single place either. In the Philippines, "Happy Hour" can happen at any hour, anywhere – just as long as you have a group of people to share in that happiness.

Much like the food and drink found in German biergartens, Japanese *izakaya*, and English pubs, Filipino pulutan is more than simple snacks served with beer; it's a way of life, a way of sharing experiences with friends and family over great food and great beverages.

BEER IS IN MY BLOOD

As an imbiber, my tastes have always leaned towards beer. And I mean always. In fact, I have very vivid childhood memories of sitting on my father's lap at many a family gathering (or maybe it was just one, who knows?) and him tilting his beer can to my lips so I could get the tiniest toddler taste of his Budweiser. Don't be alarmed—it was always just a small sip. And I turned out fine. What can I say? It was the '80s.

If there's one thing my Dad did, it was to instill in me a great appreciation for beer, Budweiser and all. In fact, today I'm a bona fide Certified Cicerone®. What's a Cicerone, you ask? Well, in very general terms, the Cicerone Certification Program® is very similar to the wine world's Court of Master Sommeliers in that there are four levels of expertise: Certified Beer Server® (general knowledge of beer service and styles), Certified Cicerone (professional beer expertise and tasting skills), Advanced Cicerone® (true beer bad asses), and Master Cicerone® (untouchable beer G.O.A.T.s with grizzled beards and widened bellies).

I won't bore you with the details of becoming a Certified Cicerone; suffice it to say that I underwent hundreds of hours studying beer styles, history, flavors, evaluation, ingredients and the brewing process, as well as the intricacies of pairing beer with food. Not to mention having to taste hundreds of different beers (tough gig, I know). And I'm still learning – always learning – just as I am with Filipino food.

So with my experience in cooking and writing about Filipino food and flavors, combined with my growing knowledge of beer tasting and pairing, I'm able to give very specific suggestions for which beers I think go best with which recipes in this cookbook. It's not exactly a super power, but at the very least it's a great parlor trick.

PICKING UP WHERE WE LEFT OFF . . .

There's a small pulutan chapter toward the end of my first book, *The Adobo Road Cookbook*, where I provided a handful of cocktail and pulutan recipes. I always wished there were more.

It was while writing that chapter and developing those recipes that I became completely obsessed with Filipino pulutan. After all, craft beer and craft cocktails were always a passion of mine as a food writer, and I even had a bit of wine experience from working for a short time at one of the first Filipino-owned wineries in the US. Pulutan was right in my wheelhouse: Filipino food + alcoholic beverages = I'm all in! So with that winning equation, I knew that I wanted to expand beyond the pulutan chapter in my first cookbook. And here we are now.

ABOUT THE RECIPES IN THIS COOKBOOK

This is my personal take on pulutan based on how I like to cook, what I like to eat and what I like to serve guests visiting my home. At a time where Filipino food is being elevated, deconstructed, resurrected, praised and enjoyed by a wider and wider audience, it was important for me to not only showcase tried-and-true pulutan standards, but to also move forward by creating dishes anew, combining different techniques, but *always* using Filipino ingredients and highlighting Filipino flavors.

ABOUT THE BEER PAIRINGS IN THIS BOOK

Almost every recipe in this cookbook (with the exception of those found in the sauces and cocktails chapters) has its own drink pairing section entitled UMINOM, which means "to drink." And within every UMINOM section, I list at least one beer pairing for you to try with the corresponding recipe. Wherever appropriate, I also provide suggestions for wines and

cocktails. But since beer is my strong suit, and because beer is most often enjoyed with pulutan in the Philippines, every recipe gets a beer suggestion.

MODERATION AND SAN MIGUEL

"True celebration is of the spirit, and needs no spirits to make it lively."
— Doreen G. Fernandez

Although the loose definition of pulutan is "things you eat while drinking alcohol," that doesn't mean you have to have a beer, a cocktail or a glass of wine in hand to enjoy the recipes in this cookbook. All of these pulutan recipes are delicious, with or without an alcoholic beverage. And it goes without saying, but if you are going to be drinking, you should do so in moderation. Pulutan is meant to soften the blow of liquor in the belly; it's not a green light to just start pounding sixers of San Miguel.

Speaking of which, the San Miguel Corporation, whose flagship product is San Miguel beer, is the single largest corporation in all of the Philippines—which explains why San Miguel beer is so ubiquitous there. But there is choice. In this day and age there are more and better craft-beer alternatives to industrial beer, and this is even evident with the many small craft breweries opening up all over the Philippines.

Now, just because I have a fancy craft beer certification doesn't necessarily mean that I'm dismissing San Miguel beer outright. I realize San Miguel has a nostalgic place in every Filipino's heart, mine included. The suggestions in the UMINOM sections are just that: suggestions. Taste is subjective, so when in doubt, drink a San Miguel; it'll feel like home. In fact, whenever I suggest a "pale lager" in any of my recipes, that's my subtle wink and signal for you to pick up a cold San Miguel.

But during this new era of Filipino chefs lifting up Filipino cuisine with the best of ingredients, why not lift up the drink selection as well?

So, are you ready for some pulutan? Let's get cooking, let's get eating, and let's get drinking! *Mabuhay! Tagay! Barik! Agbiag!* Cheers!

PREFERRED IMPLEMENTS FOR PULUTAN PREPARATION

Though I do have my fair share of fancy kitchen gizmos and gadgetry, you won't see mention of any sous vide machines, vacuum sealers, stand mixers or pressure cookers within these cookbook pages. They simply aren't needed here. Making pulutan is as rustic and down-home as cooking can get, so you are likely to already have everything you need to prep and cook your way through this book. Here is a list of the equipment and tools I recommend.

BARWARE

You don't need to be a pro bartender to make great cocktails at home. All you need are some basic bar tools like the essentials I list here.

BARSPOON

I have a confession to make: I do not own a barspoon. I have another confession: I don't even use a spoon to stir my cocktails – I use a chopstick! Yes, a chopstick. (Gasp!) Alert the bartender police! Although a chopstick can't quite twirl a tin of ice like a barspoon can, it's long enough to reach the bottom of a tin or mixing glass, and sturdy enough to quickly circulate the liquid and ice within that tin or mixing glass – which is good enough for me, and probably good enough for you, too.

COCKTAIL PICKS

Cocktail picks aren't just for spearing garnishes in your drinks; they're also great for picking up appetizers when you don't want to use your fingers. And yes, you can use cocktail umbrellas for spearing appetizers too.

Cocktail picks

COCKTAIL SHAKER

Although the pros use a two-piece Boston shaker (the kind with a shaking tin inverted over a mixing glass), I've had the same three-piece cobbler shaker since I was in college. Because it was a gift, I never had the heart to upgrade it. And I've never had any reason to – its stainless-steel tin, built-in strainer, and tight-fitting lid have been more than sufficient in my home bar for over 20 years now.

JIGGER/MEASURING CUP

Eyeballing the rum in a Rum and Coke is fine. But when mixing a cocktail a bit more complex than that, you can't really screw with the proportions; otherwise you'll end up with an imbalance. That's why I swear by my OXO mini angled measuring cup. It has a ¼ cup (65 ml) capacity, with markings for tablespoons, ounces, and milliliters. So when a recipe calls for 1½ ounces (45 ml) of rum and ¼ ounce (7 ml) of simple syrup, I know my tiny measuring cup will keep me honest and accurate.

MUDDLER

This hefty wooden pestle is great for gently mashing herbs, citrus rinds and even chili peppers in order to extract and express their essential oils and flavors. Look for a wooden muddler that is untreated and unvarnished, and long enough to reach the bottom of a pint glass.

BLENDER

This is as high-tech as it gets for me when it comes to pulutan prep. A large-capacity, high-horsepower blender is ideal for crushing ice for blended margaritas, whipping up milkshakes and smoothies and rendering lumpy sauces smooth.

CAST-IRON AND CARBON-STEEL PANS

To me, well-seasoned cast-iron and carbon-steel pans are perhaps the most versatile cooking vessels in the kitchen. Their heat retention and practically nonstick surfaces are great for searing, frying and even for using as a hot serving vessel for sizzling *sisig* (page 76). Cast iron is heavy, great at holding heat, and relatively inexpensive. Carbon steel is lighter than cast iron; it holds heat and sears just as well, but is much more expensive than cast iron. I use both pans interchangeably.

CHEF'S KNIFE

A sharp chef's knife is perhaps the most important and essential tool you can have in your kitchen. From slicing vegetables to scaling fish to butchering meat and poultry to smashing garlic cloves, a chef's knife is the original do-it-all kitchen tool. They come in a range of lengths, from 6-inch (15-cm) Japanese *santoku* knives to 8- to 12-inch (20- to 30-cm) French-style blades; choose whichever knife feels the most comfortable in your hand.

COLANDER

I reach for a large stainless-steel colander with a wide, sturdy base anytime I need to dunk something under the cold running water of my kitchen faucet. That might include fresh fruit, fresh shellfish like crab,

Colander

Muddler

Jigger/measuring cup

Cast-iron and carbon-steel pans

Dutch oven

Oyster knife

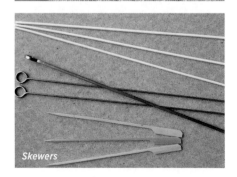
Skewers

oysters, clams or mussels, or anything else that needs rinsing. A colander is also great for draining just-blanched meats and vegetables.

DEEP-FRY THERMOMETER

Although there are other ways to check the temperature of your frying oil (e.g., dropping a grain of cooked rice into the oil to see if it sizzles), a deep-fry thermometer takes the guesswork out of frying and allows you to better control and maintain the desired frying temperature. It's also inexpensive and easy to store – all the more reason to own one.

DUTCH OVEN

I own an enameled 6-quart (6-liter) Dutch oven that I use for everything from making stocks, stews, and soups to using as a deep-frying vessel. Besides being a versatile cooking tool, it also looks nice enough to use as a serving dish.

KITCHEN SHEARS

A good, hefty pair of shears can be a true workhorse in the kitchen. I use mine for handily cutting out the backs of whole chickens, trimming herbs, cutting bacon into ribbons, and even trimming straws for Tiki drinks. Choose two-piece shears that can be completely separated for easy cleaning.

OYSTER KNIFE

Although an oyster knife isn't good for much other than opening oysters, it's the only tool for that job. So if you enjoy eating fresh oysters at home like I do, it's a must-have. An oyster knife should have a dull,

thick, sturdy blade with a handle that won't slip in your hand. For tips on shucking oysters, see page 18.

PARING KNIFE

For tasks that may be too small for a full-sized chef's knife – mincing shallots or garlic, slicing calamansi limes in half, or quartering mushrooms – a paring knife is the more efficient choice. The blade, which is between 2 and 4 inches (5–10 cm) in length, should be kept sharp at all times.

RIMMED BAKING SHEET AND WIRE RACK

I use these aluminum pans (also called jellyroll pans, cookie sheets, or half-sheets) for everything from baking cookies to setting under pies in the oven to catch drips. Lined with paper towels, a rimmed baking sheet makes for a great resting place for foods like *lumpia* when they come out of the deep fryer. Lined with foil, it makes for a great staging area for seasoning and prepping meats.

You should also have a wire rack that fits right inside your rimmed baking sheet. It's useful for holding battered items ready for the fryer, resting just-seared steaks, or for keeping a cut of meat like pork belly from sitting in its own juices as it roasts in the oven.

SKEWERS

As you'll see in Chapter 6, "Off the Grill," there are quite a few recipes for meat on sticks. Here, then, are my recommendations for the sticks on which to skewer said meat. Old-school 12-inch

(30-cm) bamboo skewers are cheap and easy to find; just make sure you soak them in water for at least 30 minutes before grilling to keep them from burning too fast. For something a bit more durable, I like 12-inch (30-cm) flat stainless steel skewers. You can use these metal skewers over and over again, and since they're flat, food will stay put and won't spin around. For grilling smaller food items like shrimp, I like to use shorter 6- to 7-inch (15- to 18-cm) flat bamboo skewers with a handle on one end that makes them easy to pick up.

Sieve

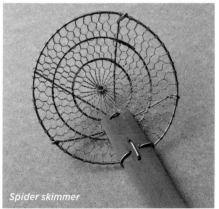

Spider skimmer

SMALL FINE-MESH SIEVE

I usually set a small sieve directly on top of a measuring cup, then squeeze calamansi juice into it to catch the seeds. I also use a small sieve to double-strain a shaken cocktail so that no stray ice chips make their way into my drink.

SPIDER SKIMMER

Primarily used for pulling fried items out of hot oil, a bamboo spider skimmer with a steel mesh basket is also great for draining small quantities of noodles and blanched vegetables or plucking hard-boiled eggs from boiling water.

TONGS

Spring-loaded stainless-steel tongs are a heat-proof extension of my hands. I own three sizes of tongs: a 16-inch (40-cm) pair for grilling, a 12-inch (30-cm) pair for keeping my distance from hot items in the oven or from scorching-hot pans on the stovetop, and a more maneuverable 9-inch (23-cm) pair that I seem to use for everything else. If you are to have just one pair of tongs, though, a 12-inch (30-cm) spring-loaded pair would be the most versatile.

VEGETABLE PEELER

Let's face it. Most of us don't have the knife skills to peel an apple or potato with a paring knife. That's where the convenience of vegetable peelers comes in: making quick work of peeling the skins off of any and all fruits and veggies. Vegetable peelers are also fantastic for

cocktail prep, allowing you to get just the right amount of citrus rind for the twist that your tipple needs.

WOK

Like the Chinese, Filipinos use the wok (called a *kawali* in the Philippines) for deep-frying, stir-frying, and steaming. A large 14-inch (36-cm) carbon-steel wok with a flat bottom is not only inexpensive, but is the perfect shape for most home stovetops. Choose one with a long heat-proof handle on one side and a shorter helper handle on the other. Although most woks come with a metal wok spatula, I prefer to use a long-handled wooden spoon when stir-frying in my wok. The handle stays cool and is long enough to keep my hand away from the blazing-hot wok.

Wok

DON'T SWEAT THESE TECHNIQUES

In this section, I hope to arm you with basic tips and techniques that will not only help you become a bit more efficient in the kitchen, but will also hopefully make you a better all-around cook. Although there are a few illustrated recipe-specific "how-tos" sprinkled throughout this cookbook (e.g., How to Roll Lumpia, page 73), the how-tos I provide below are more general techniques you should have in your back pocket for everyday Filipino cooking beyond the recipes in this book.

Lastly, I close out this section with some beer pairing basics and tips on cooking with beer. Having a basic foundation and knowledge of a beer's individual characteristics and flavors goes a long way toward understanding how beer will interact with food, and how those characteristics and flavors can change with cooking.

HOW TO SQUEEZE, MEASURE AND STORE CALAMANSI JUICE

If I'm adding a finishing spritz of fresh calamansi juice over some noodles or grilled fish, I simply cut a calamansi in half, pick the seeds out with a paring knife, and give the calamansi a squeeze. But if I need to actually measure the juice for a recipe, I use the method below – it makes for easier seed removal and accurate measuring beyond a simple spritz.

For cocktail recipes and others that only call for small quantities of juice, I find that 4 or 5 calamansi limes usually yield about 1 tablespoon (½ ounce) of juice. For larger quantities, I've found that 1 pound (500 g) of calamansi limes often yields between ¾ cup (185 ml) to 1 cup (250 ml) of juice. I'm sure there's a math problem in there somewhere.

1. Using a sharp knife, cut the desired quantity of calamansi limes in half.

Place a small fine-mesh sieve directly on top of a measuring cup. (If I'm measuring for cocktails, I usually use a small cocktail jigger. If I'm measuring a larger quantity, I use a standard large measuring cup.)

2. Squeeze the calamansi limes over the sieve so that the juice passes through into the measuring cup, but the seeds are caught in the sieve. Continue squeezing limes until you have enough juice for your recipe. Discard the seeds and the rinds.

3. If you aren't going to use the calamansi juice right away, you can freeze it in ice-cube trays. Once the calamansi cubes are completely frozen, transfer them to a resealable plastic storage bag and store them in the freezer until they are needed.

HOW TO PREPARE LEMONGRASS

Be sure that your chef's knife is sharp when preparing lemongrass, as the woody texture of the stalk can be tough for dull knives to cut through.

1. The whole length of a lemongrass stalk provides aroma, but only the tender bottom portion is edible.
2. Begin by using a chef's knife to cut off the bottom ½ inch (1 cm) or so of the lemongrass stalk. Remove and discard the outermost layers of the stalk.
3. Cut off the bottom 4 to 6 inches (10 to 15 cm) of the stalk; discard the darker green upper stalk.
4. Using a mallet or the spine of your chef's knife, pound the remaining lemongrass to lightly bruise it. Pounding the lemongrass makes it easier to cut and also helps to release some of the essential oils. At this point, you can cut the lemongrass as needed for your recipes. Slice, dice, finely mince, or use the entire piece.

HOW TO PREPARE BITTER MELON

Most of the bitterness in a bitter melon lies in the spongy white pith and seeds within, so cutting the green gourd open and scraping away its insides is always a good idea. Don't worry; bitter melon is still plenty bitter even without its pith and seeds.

1. Trim off the ends of the bitter melon with a sharp knife, then slice in half lengthwise.
2. Using a spoon or a melon baller, scrape out and discard the seeds and white pith from the center of the bitter melon. Scrape out as much of the pith as possible without damaging the green flesh.
3. Here's how your bitter melon should look once you've scraped out the pith and seeds.
4. Cut the bitter melon into ¼-inch (6-mm) slices.

HOW TO SHUCK AN OYSTER

Although I've opened my fair share of fresh oysters with nothing more than a butter knife, using an oyster knife is much easier and safer. You'll need a clean kitchen towel to keep the oyster to be opened in place, as well as to protect your non-knife-holding hand. Before opening any oysters, you should scrub and rinse them under cold running water in your kitchen sink. This will reduce the chance of getting any mud or dirt on the inside of the oyster during opening.

1. Place a scrubbed oyster, curved side down and flat side up, on a clean kitchen towel that has been folded lengthwise into thirds.
2. Using your non-knife-holding hand, grab one end of the towel and fold it over the oyster so that only the hinge end of the oyster is exposed. Your thumb and hand should also be protected by the towel in case your oyster knife should slip.
3. Insert the oyster knife into the exposed hinge end of the oyster and push, working the knife back and forth until you feel it slide between the top and bottom oyster shells. This may take a little bit of effort, but you shouldn't be forcing your way into the oyster with the knife. You are simply trying to work the tip of the knife far enough between the oyster shells so that you can use the knife as leverage.
4. Once you feel the tip of the knife slide between the oyster shells, twist the knife to pop the top shell open. Again, you shouldn't have to force this; if you have enough leverage it should be relatively easy to pop open the top shell.
5. Before proceeding any further, remove the knife from the shell and wipe it clean on the kitchen towel in case there was any dirt or mud in the hinge of the oyster. Reinsert the knife and continue to pry open the shell, sliding and scraping your blade underneath the upper shell to separate it from the oyster. Be careful to not spill any of the delicious liquid still inside the shell.
6. You should now be able to easily remove and discard the top shell from the oyster. The oyster inside should look and smell clean, and the liquid should be clear. If anything smells off, throw away the whole thing. Slide your knife underneath the oyster to sever it from the bottom shell. Now the oyster is ready for slurping.

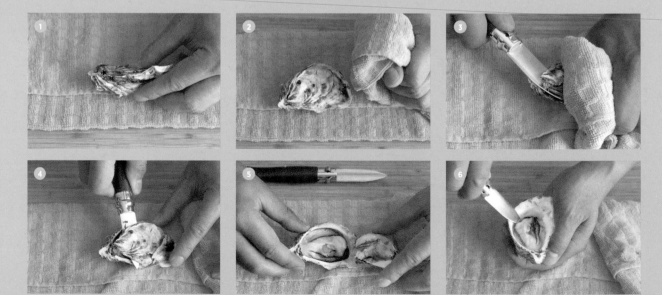

BEER PAIRING BASICS

If you'd like to expand and explore other beers beyond the pairings I suggest in this book (and you should!), just remember: complement, contrast and cut. These "three Cs" will serve as a sort of basic road map for you when navigating all the possible interactions between beer and food.

COMPLEMENT Like the food you eat, the beer you drink encompasses a number of different flavors and aromas. Keep that in mind when choosing a beer for any given dish, and look for characteristics in the beer that will harmonize with the characteristics of the food. For instance, the tropical fruit flavors like pineapple and mango in many American IPAs will enhance the pineapple glaze on a grilled pork belly skewer. But don't stop there. The smoky flavors in a smoked porter, or especially in a German Rauchbier, would also help bring out the smoke on the grilled pork.

CONTRAST The opposite of complementing, this can be a bit harder to pull off in a beer pairing. Choose characteristics in a beer that will simultaneously contrast with and accentuate the flavors and aromas in a dish, and vice versa. A classic example of a contrasting beer pairing is raw oysters paired with Irish stout. The dry bitterness and roasty malt flavors of the stout play very well against the sweet and briny flavors of a fresh oyster. Having a Filipino-style adobo for dinner? The peppery notes in a Saison would be a welcome contrast to the soy and vinegar sauce in the adobo.

CUT This aspect of beer pairing refers more to mouthfeel than flavor or aroma. Carbonation, bitterness and acidity in beer can all help to "cut" through or cleanse the palate of fat, richness or oiliness in food. The high carbonation of a Belgian Witbier can cut through the richness of avocado, for example, while the moderate bitterness of a Belgian Dubbel is enough to cut through the fat of a grilled lamb chop.

INTENSITY Okay, not one of the three Cs above, but just as important to note. You always want to match intensities in beer and food – you don't want one to overpower the other. A rich chocolate cake with chocolate icing makes sense when paired with the robust coffee notes, roast and high alcohol of a Russian imperial stout. But if that same cake was paired with the light, clean, sprightly flavors of a pale Pilsner, then the cake's intensity would win out, and your taste buds would definitely lose.

The "three Cs" plus intensity above are just a starting point or reference for you to begin exploring beer and food pairings. The good news is that the more beers you drink and the more you eat, the more flavor connections you will make, and the more experience you will gain – just make sure to mix in some cardio if you can.

COOKING WITH BEER

Beyond the suggested beer pairings in each "UMINOM" sidebar in this book, there are also a number of recipes that call for beer as an ingredient. When beer is used for cooking, it typically serves as a more flavorful replacement for water and other liquids. I use beer for everything, including steaming (Beer-Steamed Blue Crabs, page 87; Beer-Steamed Clams and Spam, page 94), battering (Corn-Dogged Quail Eggs, page 54), and marinating (Beer-Marinated Chicken Skewers with Shrimp Paste Rub, page 104), to name just a few.

But before you start cooking with beer, know that applying heat to beer will concentrate the flavors in that beer. This concentration of flavors can be both good and bad:

Be wary when using intensely hopped beers (like IPAs) in cooking, as the hoppy bitterness will intensify and can become harsh and astringent. I actually use this to my advantage in my IPA *papaitan* recipe (Beef, Tripe and Ginger Soup, page 90); the Filipino stew is traditionally very, very bitter.

Likewise, the astringent, acidic, bitter and burnt flavors in a roasty beer like a porter or a stout will also intensify with cooking. Again, I use this to my advantage in Heavenly Beer and Peanut Brittle (page 110) where the roasty bitterness of a Doppelbock is used to contrast the sweet caramel of the sugars in the brittle.

Applying heat to beer isn't your only option, though. While heat concentrates flavor, it also serves to cook off more volatile (easily evaporated) aromas like spice, citrus, herb, fruit, etc. Which means you can use beer in its more natural uncooked state for marinades, salad dressings, dips and even desserts like ice creams or popsicles (page 113).

THE PULUTAN PANTRY

If you're going to prepare delicious pulutan, you need to have a well-stocked pulutan pantry. The items listed here are called for most frequently throughout this cookbook; luckily, they can be easily found at your friendly neighborhood supermarket, Asian market, or Filipino market. Stock up on these ingredients, and you'll be ready to feed your guests – no matter how hungry and thirsty they may be!

BEER Of course, this is the first pantry item listed! Throughout this book, there are suggested beers that you can pair, drink and enjoy with each finished dish. But beers aren't only good for drinking – they're good for cooking too, so a number of recipes call for the use of beer as an ingredient. In these cases, I usually specify the preferred style of beer to be used in that recipe (e.g., an India pale ale for the *papaitan* on page 90; a Doppelbock for the peanut brittle on page 110).

As a general rule of thumb, you can choose to cook with a cheaper, more accessible industrial beer if you don't have or can't find the specific craft beer that I specify in a given recipe. In fact, I often have a six-pack of cheap beer in my pantry

that I specifically use for cooking – Filipino San Miguel beer fits this bill nicely, as does Budweiser, Pabst Blue Ribbon, and the like. While these commercial beers won't deliver the same depth of character as their microbrewed counterparts, they will still add plenty of flavor to the finished dish.

BITTER MELON (AMPALAYA) Bitter melon (also known as bitter gourd) is pale green in color with an irregular wrinkly surface; its flavor is, indeed, quite bitter. This member of the squash family is reputed to have an abundance of health benefits and is used in dishes throughout the Philippines, though seen most often in the northern part of the archipelago.

CALAMANSI Calamansi limes (also called kalamansi or calmondin) are small citrus fruits that have the fragrance of mandarin oranges and the sour citrus flavor of lemons

Calamansi

and limes. Calamansi are about 1 inch (2.5 cm) in diameter and range in color from green to orange. A squeeze, a squirt or a spritz of calamansi juice brightens up any dish — from noodles to soups to grilled meats and fish. Calamansi juice is also great mixed in desserts and cocktails. Calamansi can sometimes be found at Asian markets or even at local farmers' markets, so if you ever encounter these fragrant orbs, be sure to buy in bulk! I've found that 1 pound (500 g) of calamansi limes generally yields between ¾ cup (185 ml) and 1 cup (250 ml) of juice. But the best way to ensure a steady supply of these wonderful limes is to grow your own tree in your backyard. Potted calamansi trees can often be found in the nursery department of hardware stores; small ones can be purchased online as well. And of course, fresh lemon juice or lime juice can always be substituted for calamansi juice.

CANOLA OIL
Because of its relatively high smoke point and neutral flavor, I most often reach for canola oil in my everyday cooking. Excellent in simple salad dressings and for sautéing, stir-frying or deep-frying, canola oil is a truly versatile cooking oil.

COCONUT MILK
Coconut milk is made from the shredded flesh of mature brown coconuts that is mixed with water and pressed. Coconut milk made from the first pressing is thicker and richer; subsequent pressings produce thinner, less flavorful milk. Although freshly made coconut milk is preferred in the Philippines, canned unsweetened coconut milk can be used with equally wonderful results. I prefer the Chaokoh and Aroy-D brands of canned coconut milk from Thailand, as both are consistently flavorful and creamy. When

working with canned coconut milk, always give the can a vigorous shake before opening; after opening the can, use a spoon to stir the coconut milk again before adding it to your dish.

COCONUT OIL
Because it is generally highly processed, treated with chemicals, and deodorized, refined coconut oil lacks any coconut flavor or aroma, but it is great for high-temperature cooking due to its relatively high smoke point.

Although it has a lower smoke point than refined coconut oil, cold-pressed, unrefined virgin coconut oil is my preferred coconut oil, since it retains its natural tropical flavor and fragrance. It's great for baking, quick sautéing and adding a distinct coconut taste and aroma to dishes.

It should also be noted that coconut oil remains solid at room temperature, but like butter, it can be quickly and easily melted in the microwave for easier measuring.

DISTILLED COCONUT NECTAR (LAMBANOG)
Native to the Philippines, *lambanog* (also marketed as coconut arrack, coconut vodka or coconut wine) is a high-proof spirit distilled from the sap or nectar of a coconut tree flower. If that

sounds complicated, that's because it is. Collecting the nectar requires a person to climb to the top of a coconut tree, slice the coconut flower with a very sharp knife, and then catch the nectar in a special bamboo container slung across the shoulders. The nectar is then carried down, cooked and distilled into lambanog. Although it is usually enjoyed as-is, the resulting beverage can be flavored with prunes, raisins, spices or native fruits, depending on the whims of the distiller.

Although lambanog has traditionally been more akin to American moonshine, good-quality commercial examples have become more widely available in recent years. Brands like Infanta and Vuqo can be easily found at Asian or Filipino markets, as well as ordered online. Commercially made lambanog is similar to vodka in that it is generally colorless and tasteless, save for a high-alcohol kick.

DRIED RED CHILI FLAKES
I use these spicy flakes to add a hint of heat to dishes when I don't have fresh chili peppers on hand—though sometimes I use both at the same time to achieve different layers of spice.

DRIED SHRIMP Known as *hibe* in the Philippines, these tiny dried shrimp, no bigger than a thumbnail, are added to soups and stews for an umami boost.

EDAM CHEESE Known as *queso de bola* in the Philippines, this savory cheese is often grated onto Filipino desserts as a salty counterpoint, but it's also great in grilled-cheese sandwiches (page 55), or shredded onto spicy chili (page 84). Gouda is a fine substitute if you can't find Edam.

FERMENTED FISH/SHRIMP PASTE (BAGOONG) A very pungent and salty condiment that can be made from tiny fish or tiny shrimp. The most commonly available type of shrimp paste available in the States are *bagoong alamang* (also labeled as shrimp fry) and *ginisang bagoong* (labeled as sautéed shrimp paste). They are used to add salt and savory umami to dishes. Because it has a fewer number of items in its ingredients list and lacks the artificial bright pink color of bagoong alamang, I prefer to use ginisang bagoong in my cooking, though both are good options.

FISH SAUCE (PATIS): Ubiquitous throughout Southeast Asia, fish sauce is an essential ingredient in Filipino cooking. It is used to impart not only saltiness, but

savoriness (umami) as well. Fish sauce is made from fermented anchovies, and although it has a very pungent aroma, if used properly it will not make your food taste fishy. It can be used to season cooked dishes, and may also be used as a dipping sauce. When shopping, look for fish sauce that is light amber in color and labeled as being made from the first extraction of the fish. Keep in mind that the saltiness in fish sauce varies with the brand. Rufina is a good Filipino brand, but Three Crabs (Vietnam), Red Boat (Vietnam) and Squid (Thailand) are fine as well.

GINGER (LUYA) Properly speaking a rhizome rather than a root, ginger imparts a bright, sweet, zesty and spicy flavor that I love in nearly everything I cook. When shopping for ginger, look for smooth, tight skin without any blemishes. Wrinkles are a sign of an older and more fibrous root.

GINGER BEER Don't let the name fool you. Ginger beer contains no alcohol, and generally speaking, is similar to ginger ale but has a spicier, more pronounced ginger flavor. It's not only great in cocktails like the Barrelman Buck (page 39), but it's also wonderful when used as part of a marinade/barbecue glaze like in the Liempo-Cue (page 106). I prefer Reed's brand of ginger beer. If you can't find ginger beer, regular ginger ale is a suitable substitute.

GREEN MANGO Green mangoes are simply firm, unripe mangoes prized for their sour flavor. Usually sliced and served with bagoong fermented fish paste for a salty-sour snack, green mangoes can also provide texture and tartness to raw salads. Look for green mangoes that are very firm and have a pale green skin. You can find green mangoes at Asian markets.

LEMONGRASS (TANGLAD)

Lemongrass is an aromatic and edible species of grass that lends a beautiful lemon flavor and aroma without any acid. The whole length of a lemongrass stalk provides aroma, but only the tender bottom portion of the stalk is edible. To prepare lemongrass for use, see "How to Prepare Lemongrass," page 17.

MANGO

Although unripe green mangoes are prized for their sourness in the Philippines, soft ripe sweet mangoes are beloved and even lusted for in the Philippines. The mangoes labeled as "Manila Mangoes" sold here in the States are often actually grown in Mexico. Despite this misleading nomenclature, you can still find a great variety of mangoes in many grocery stores. When choosing mangoes, look for fruit with smooth, taut skin. When ripe, the mango should feel heavy for its size, and it should smell sweet and deeply fruity. Lastly, give the mango a squeeze — it should be slightly soft and yield a bit to your fingertips.

PAN DE SAL

Despite its salty sounding name, this slightly sweet Filipino bread roll isn't salty at all. Best when hot out of the oven, freshly baked pan de sal can be found at any Filipino bakery, but pre-packaged rolls can also easily be found at Asian and Filipino markets. Traditionally slathered with a little butter and fruit jam and eaten with coffee, pan de sal is also a great dinner roll for sopping up sauces, or toasted and topped with avocados (page 51) or grilled tomatoes (page 52). Hawaiian sweet rolls are a good substitute if you can't find pan de sal.

PANKO BREAD CRUMBS

Because of their jagged, irregular shape, these Japanese bread crumbs deliver great crunch and texture when used as a coating for fried foods such as Fried Green Mangoes (page 68), or as a crunchy topping for Spicy Deviled Eggs (page 48). Panko bread crumbs are widely available and can be found at most supermarkets.

POMELO (SUHA):

Native to Southeast Asia, the pomelo is a large citrus fruit that looks very similar to a grapefruit. The pomelo tastes very similar to grapefruit, but is generally sweeter and lacks any pronounced bitterness. The fruit also has a very thick rind with white spongy pith, and there are tough membranes between each segment. Pomelo can be used in the Gin Pom Cocktail (page 37), as well as in Gin, Pomelo and Shrimp Cocktail (page 62). To peel and segment a pomelo, see page 63.

PRAWN CRACKERS

Also known as shrimp chips or *kropek*, these light, airy, crispy puffs are popular snacks throughout Southeast Asia. These shrimp-flavored chips make a great pulutan all by themselves, but I also like to use them for scooping up my Gin, Pomelo and Shrimp Cocktail (page 62),

or to add texture to Spicy Sizzling Squid (page 76). Prawn crackers can be found at any Asian market.

SAMBAL OELEK

Though it's not a traditional ingredient in Filipino cuisine, I love using this spicy Indonesian chili paste in marinades because it mixes into liquids easily and provides a convenient form of heat and spice. Sambal oelek chili paste can be found in small plastic jars in Asian markets, as well as in some supermarkets — either in the Asian aisle or right next to other commercial hot sauces.

SEA SALT

The Philippines has its own variety of artisanal and locally harvested sea salts that can rival those produced in other parts of the world. You can find gourmet Philippine sea salt in upscale markets and from online retailers. My supply of Philippine sea salt, however, comes from the wet market in Badoc, Ilocos Norte, in the northern region of the Philippines. My mother tends to visit our family there at least once a year, so I make sure that she brings me back a 3- to 5-pound (1.5- to 2-kg) bag of Philippine sea salt from our preferred *suki* (vendor) at that specific wet market. (Yes, my mother is basically a salt mule for me.) And because I use it interchangeably with kosher salt, I have a huge surplus of Philippine sea salt in my cupboard.

SHALLOTS

These aromatic bulbs are similar to onions, but smaller in size and milder in flavor. Shallots can be eaten raw or sautéed along with garlic and ginger in many Filipino recipes.

SMOKED SPANISH PAPRIKA (PIMENTÓN)

Made from ground chili peppers that are first dried and smoked over oak fires, smoked Spanish paprika lends a wonderfully rich and smoky flavor and aroma when sprinkled onto meats, poultry and fish. It can be found in the spice aisle of most grocery stores, or ordered online.

SOY SAUCE

Nearly ubiquitous in Asian cooking, soy sauce not only adds saltiness to dishes, but also lends a rich and savory umami flavor as well. Because it's so widely available, and because I like its

flavor, I usually have a large jug of low-sodium Kikkoman soy sauce in my pantry, though the Filipino Swan brand of soy sauce is also great.

SPAM

To me, there are two types of people: those that love Spam, and those who have never actually tried Spam but claim to hate it. Obviously, I belong to the pro-Spam camp and I have a can of the processed pork product in my pantry at all times. Sliced into steaks or diced into small cubes, Spam adds a salty, meaty and delicious flavor to any dish. Although there are over a dozen different types of flavored Spam, including Jalapeño, Bacon and even the Filipino-targeted Tocino variety, I stick to the classic original Spam in the blue can.

THAI CHILI PEPPERS (SILING LABUYO)

Also known as Thai bird or bird's-eye chili peppers, these small, fiery pods are the spice of choice in the Philippines. They can be thinly sliced and tossed raw into dipping sauces, or added to cooked dishes for added spice.

TOFU

Ranging from soft and silken to hard and extra-firm, tofu is a great vegetarian protein option in many dishes. Usually stored in water, tofu should be drained and patted dry with paper towels before using.

UBE FLOUR

Ube is the popular purple sweet yam that is used in a wide variety of sweet Filipino desserts. Ube flour is simply dehydrated and pulverized purple sweet yam. Ube flour does not add much of the sweetness and flavor that fresh ube does, but it lends a beautiful purple hue and a cornmeal-like texture to whatever dish it's used in, from fried calamari (page 70) to churros (page 114). Ube flour can be easily found in Asian markets.

VINEGARS

In the Philippines, a variety of locally sourced artisanal vinegars are made from the fermented nectar, sap or juices of different plants or fruits grown in the surrounding areas. Luckily, many of these vinegars can be found at Asian markets. Datu Puti, Tropics, and Masagana are all good brands from the Philippines.

The vinegars I list here generally hover between 4 and 5 percent acidity. And while each of them provides a different nuanced flavor, they can generally be substituted for one another in the recipes in this cookbook. Also, for each recipe that uses a Filipino vinegar, I do provide a more accessible alternative, such as apple cider vinegar, white distilled vinegar or unseasoned rice vinegar.

PALM VINEGAR (SUKANG PAOMBONG)

Filipino palm vinegar is made from the fermented sap of the Nipa palm. It is named for Paombong, a region of the Philippines that is known for its palm vinegar. *Sukang paombong* is cloudy white in appearance and has subtle notes of lemon and citrus.

COCONUT VINEGAR (SUKANG TUBA)

Filipino coconut-sap vinegar, made from the fermented sap of a coconut tree, is perhaps the most commonly used vinegar in the Philippines due to the abundance of coconuts there. *Sukang tuba* is also cloudy white in appearance, with a slightly sweet smell. Despite its provenance, coconut vinegar lacks any coconut flavor or aroma; it's very pungent and sour. You can find coconut vinegar in Asian markets, and organic varieties can also be found (for a higher price) in health food stores.

DARK SUGARCANE VINEGAR (SUKANG ILOCO)

Filipino cane vinegar from the Ilocos region of the Philippines is a byproduct of the Ilocano sugarcane wine known as *basi*. Basi is made by pressing juice from sugarcane, cooking it to a thick molasses consistency, and then placing the syrup in clay jars. The bark from the *duhat* (Java plum) tree is added to the clay jars as a flavoring and fermenting agent. The molasses first turns into alcoholic basi wine, but if left to ferment longer, it sours further and transforms into *sukang iloco* – a dark-brown vinegar with a very slight hint of sweetness to mellow and round out its sourness.

WHITE SUGARCANE VINEGAR (SUKANG MAASIM)

White sugarcane vinegar is made from fermented sugarcane syrup. The juice and sap are pressed out of the sugarcane, then cooked and left to ferment into vinegar.

Sukang maasim is only slightly cloudy, and is relatively mild in flavor. This all-purpose vinegar is good for use in everything from adobo to dipping sauces.

SAUCES, DIPS & PICKLES

Filipino food is all about personal customization. You might enjoy dipping your fried *lumpia* spring rolls into vinegar, while your drinking companions may want something on the sweeter side. To that end, no Filipino meal – even a small one taken with drinks – is complete without a selection of sauces, dips and pickles ranging from sharp and acidic to spicy and sweet, salty and savory, or all of the above.

SPICY FISH SAUCE AND CALAMANSI DIP
PATIS–MANSI

This is the *sawsawan* (sauce) you should reach for when your seafood could benefit from a touch of umami, citrus and spicy heat. Try it with Fried Smelt (page 75) or Beer-Steamed Blue Crabs (page 87).

MAKES ½ CUP (125 ML)
PREP TIME: 5 MINUTES

¼ cup (65 ml) fish sauce
¼ cup (65 ml) fresh calamansi juice or lime juice
2 or 3 Thai chili peppers, thinly sliced
¼ teaspoon freshly ground black pepper
Pinch of sugar

Whisk all ingredients together in a small bowl until well combined. Serve with fish and shellfish.

FISH SAUCE AND CALAMANSI CARAMEL PATIS–MANSI ARNIBAL

Savory and sweet, salty and sour, this thick caramel is redolent with the funk of fish sauce and the tang of calamansi. Use it on grilled fish and meat, as a savory caramel for *taho* (page 61), or as a base for a spicy glaze on chicken wings (page 80).

MAKES ABOUT ¾ CUP (180 ML)
PREP TIME: 5 MINUTES
COOK TIME: 20 MINUTES

½ cup (90 g) brown sugar
1 tablespoon water
4 tablespoons fish sauce
4 tablespoons fresh calamansi juice or lime juice, divided

Place the sugar and water in a large, heavy-bottomed saucepan over medium heat. Once the sugar completely melts and begins to darken, stir constantly until the mixture begins to bubble and thicken, 2 to 3 minutes.

Slowly whisk in the fish sauce and 3 tablespoons of the calamansi juice. The mixture will bubble furiously, so take care not to burn yourself. Continue stirring the mixture over medium heat until it is thoroughly combined and has begun to thicken into a caramel, 3 to 5 minutes more.

Remove the sauce from the heat and stir in the last tablespoon of calamansi juice. The caramel can be stored in a plastic squeeze bottle for up to a month in the refrigerator for easy drizzling and dispensing. Reheat cold caramel with 10-second intervals in the microwave as needed.

GREEN MANGO HOT SAUCE

With chili spice coming from two types of very hot peppers, this hot sauce is downright incendiary. But it's also balanced with the sweet-tartness of the green mango and umami richness from a splash of fish sauce, and it's full of complex aromatics from the shallots, garlic and beer. This sauce may be incredibly spicy, but it's also great on almost everything.

   If you want a less fiery sauce, you can remove the veins and seeds from the chili peppers. Or you can opt to substitute an equal weight of less spicy chilies for the Thai chili peppers.

MAKES ABOUT 3 CUPS (750 ML)
PREP TIME: 15 MINUTES
COOK TIME: 30 MINUTES

1 large unripe green mango (about 12 oz/350 g),
   peeled, pitted and roughly chopped
1 large shallot, roughly chopped
1 clove garlic, roughly chopped
25 to 30 red Thai chili peppers (about 1½ oz/40 g),
   deseeded if desired, roughly chopped
2 red Fresno or Jalapeño chili peppers (about 1½
   oz/40 g), deseeded if desired, roughly chopped
¾ cup (185 ml) Filipino white cane vinegar (*sukang
   maasim*)
¼ cup (65 ml) beer, preferably a pale lager
1 teaspoon fish sauce
½ teaspoon coarse sea salt

Combine all ingredients in a small pot and bring to a boil
over high heat. Reduce heat to low and simmer uncovered
for 20 to 25 minutes, until mangoes are very soft. Remove
from heat and allow to cool to room temperature. Pour
entire contents of pot into a blender and blend until
smooth. If the sauce is thicker than desired, thin with
water as needed.

GARLIC BAGOONG AIOLI

Fermented shrimp paste, or *bagoong* as it is known in the Philippines, lends a funky, salty umami hit of flavor to anything it comes into contact with. Combining pungent bagoong with a garlicky aioli makes for a full-flavored dip that's ideal for fried foods.

MAKES ABOUT 1 CUP (250 ML)
PREP TIME: 5 MINUTES

1 egg yolk
3 cloves garlic, minced
Pinch of coarse sea salt, plus more to taste
2 teaspoons fresh calamansi juice or lemon juice
1 teaspoon white Filipino cane vinegar (*sukang maasim*)
¾ cup (185 ml) canola oil
1 to 2 teaspoons fermented shrimp paste (*bagoong*)
Freshly ground black pepper, to taste

Combine the egg yolk, garlic, salt, calamansi juice and cane vinegar in a large bowl and whisk until light and frothy. Continue whisking constantly as you drizzle in a few drops of the oil to begin an emulsification. Drizzle in a few more drops of oil and continue to whisk vigorously until the mixture thickens a bit, 2 to 3 minutes.

Gradually add the remaining oil in a slow, thin stream, whisking all the while, until the mixture thickens and a mayonnaise is formed, about 3 to 5 minutes more. Add the shrimp paste to the mayonnaise and gently fold until it is evenly distributed throughout. Season to taste with salt and pepper.

The aioli will last up to a week covered in the refrigerator.

Try this addictive sauce with Fried Calamari (page 10), Fried Green Mangoes (page 68), or Crispy Oven-Roasted Pork Belly (page 92).

CITRUS-PICKLED ONIONS BURONG SIBUYAS

With a sharp onion bite and citrusy tang, these quick-pickled onions are great on everything from salads to sandwiches. But they're especially delicious as an accompaniment to rich, fatty meats, like Grilled Pork Belly Skewers (page 106).

MAKES ABOUT 1 CUP (150 G)
PREP TIME: 10 MINUTES

½ large red onion, thinly sliced (about 1 cup/150 g)
⅓ cup calamansi juice or lime juice
¼ teaspoon coarse sea salt
¼ teaspoon sugar
¼ teaspoon red chili flakes

Place all ingredients in a medium bowl and toss to combine. Cover and refrigerate for at least 2 hours before serving. Pickled onions will last up to one week in the refrigerator.

SWEET AND SHARP SHALLOT SAUCE

In addition to the salty-sour soy and vinegar base of this sauce, there is also caramelized-shallot sweetness, and a sharp onion bite from the raw shallots. Like the All-Purpose Vinegar Dip (facing page), this sauce is great on just about anything, but it's ideal with Pigs' Ear and Tofu Spring Rolls (page 72).

MAKES ABOUT 1 CUP (250 ML)
PREP TIME: 5 MINUTES
COOK TIME: 20 MINUTES

2 large shallots
1 teaspoon canola oil
1 teaspoon brown sugar
½ cup (125 ml) water (or as needed)
½ cup (125 ml) soy sauce
¼ cup (65 ml) Filipino white cane vinegar (*sukang maasim*) or plain rice vinegar

Slice the shallots thinly. Separate and chop 1 tablespoon, reserving for later.

Heat the canola oil in a large heavy-bottomed saucepan over moderately high heat. Add the sliced shallots and the brown sugar and cook, stirring frequently, until the bottom of the saucepan is covered in a brown glaze, about 5 minutes. Add 2 tablespoons of water to the pan, and stir to clean and scrape up the browned bits from the bottom of the pan. Repeat cooking, adding water, and scraping until shallots are soft, dark brown, and caramelized, 10 to 15 minutes total. If you find that the shallots are cooking too quickly and are beginning to burn, just add water, stir, and reduce the heat as needed.

Once the shallots are caramelized, transfer them to a serving dish and stir in the soy sauce and vinegar. Add the reserved 1 tablespoon of chopped raw shallots to the sauce, and serve.

MAKES ABOUT ½ CUP (125 ML)
PREP TIME: 5 MINUTES

½ cup (125 ml) Filipino vinegar, apple cider vinegar or rice vinegar
1 tablespoon minced shallots or garlic, or a combination of both
1 green onion (scallion), thinly sliced, or 2 tablespoons chopped cilantro or parsley
¼ teaspoon dried red pepper flakes or sliced Thai chili pepper
¼ teaspoon salt
¼ teaspoon freshly ground black pepper

Whisk all ingredients together in a small bowl until well combined. Serve as a dipping sauce for fried foods, grilled meat and fish, or raw fish (*kinilaw*) preparations.

ALL-PURPOSE VINEGAR DIP

Along with calamansi juice, vinegar serves as one of the primary *sawsawans*, or sauces, at the Filipino table. Every Filipino household has its own version of a vinegar dip used for everything from grilled meats and fish to fried foods and even raw fish. It can be as spartan and simple as vinegar and garlic, or it can be more of an "everything but the kitchen sink" version like the recipe you see here.

Use this recipe as a guideline, choosing whichever Filipino vinegar you wish and adding whatever chopped aromatics suit your taste buds. The main idea is to have a pungent, sour hit of flavor to cut, complement or contrast whatever you are dipping into the sauce.

IPA PICKLED BITTER MELON

Bitterness is a flavor profile favored in the Ilocos region of the northern Philippines, where bitter melon (*ampalaya*) is showcased in a number of dishes. So while pickling a bitter vegetable in a bitter beer may seem like overkill to you, it doesn't to an Ilocano like me.

    Because they have a touch of spice, incredible floral and citrus notes from the beer and a sweetness that follows the initial bitter bite, you don't have to be Ilocano to enjoy these crunchy, bittersweet pickles. They're a great foil for grilled meats and fish. They're also perfect in a martini (page 36). But if you're anything like me, you might just like eating them straight from the jar.

MAKES ABOUT A PINT (500 ML) OF PICKLES
PREP TIME: 5 MINUTES
COOK TIME: 10 MINUTES

½ lb (225 g) bitter melon, seeds and pith removed, cut into ¼ in (6 mm) thick half-moon slices

1 cup (250 ml) India pale ale

1 cup (250 ml) Filipino white cane vinegar (*sukang maasim*) or apple cider vinegar

1 teaspoon whole black peppercorns

¼ teaspoon dried red pepper flakes

2 tablespoons sugar

1 tablespoon salt

To prepare and slice the bitter melon, see page 17.

    Sterilize a pint (500 ml) jar by placing it in a pot of boiling water for 5 minutes. Remove from water and drain well. Place the bitter melon inside the jar and set aside.

    Combine remaining ingredients in a small saucepan. Bring to a boil over high heat, then reduce heat to low and simmer, stirring occasionally, until the sugar and salt dissolve, about 3 minutes. Pour the hot liquid into the jar, leaving at least ½ inch (1.25 cm) of headspace. You may not need all of the liquid. Seal the jar, allow to cool to room temperature, then store in the refrigerator for at least three days before enjoying. These pickles will keep for up to two months in the refrigerator.

LAGER PICKLED LONG BEANS

These long beans pickled in lager are the yin to the yang of the IPA-Pickled Bitter Melon. They're great for everyday snacking. When all you want is a good salty-sour pickle, this is what you should reach for.

MAKES ABOUT A PINT (500 ML) OF PICKLES
PREP TIME: 10 MINUTES
COOK TIME: 10 MINUTES

½ lb (225 g) long beans
1 teaspoon coriander seeds
1 teaspoon whole black peppercorns
1 or 2 Thai chili peppers, partially split in half lengthwise with stems still intact
1 cup (250 ml) coconut vinegar (*sukang tuba*) or white distilled vinegar
1 cup (250 ml) pale lager
2 teaspoons coarse sea salt
2 teaspoons sugar
1 clove garlic, peeled
1 bay leaf

Rinse the long beans and trim off the ends. Measure and cut them so they will fit standing on end in a pint (500 ml) jar, with at least ½ inch (1.25 cm) of headspace. Set aside.

Sterilize the jar by placing it in a pot of boiling water for 5 minutes. Remove from water and drain. Place the coriander seeds, peppercorns and chili peppers in the bottom of the clean jar. Pack as many of the trimmed beans into the jar as will fit, and set aside.

In a small saucepan, combine the vinegar, lager, salt, sugar, garlic and bay leaf. Bring to a boil over high heat, then reduce heat to low and simmer, stirring occasionally, for 3 minutes. Pour the hot liquid into the jar, leaving at least ½ inch (1.25 cm) of headspace. You may not need all of the liquid. Slide the garlic and bay leaf down into the jar, then seal the jar. Allow to cool to room temperature, then store in the refrigerator for at least 3 days before enjoying. Will keep refrigerated for up to 2 months.

CHAPTER ONE

DOWN THE HATCH
COCKTAILS &
ELIXIRS

Potent potables are paramount to pulutan.
Without them, the Filipino bar snacks
in this book would just be snacks. And
that's okay, but definitely not as fun. So in
addition to all the beer pairings and wine
suggestions I've included throughout this
book, I'm providing additional alcohol
opportunities with the cocktails in this
section – all in the name of fun, of course.

BITTER, LOW-DOWN DIRTY MARTINI

If you're a regular imbiber of dirty martinis like I am, you'll want to give this variation a try. Instead of the usual cocktail-olive garnish and splash of olive brine, this version features a slice of my IPA Pickled Bitter Melon and a splash of its bitter IPA brine. These may seem like inconsequential substitutions, but the IPA brine delivers citrus and herbal notes from the beer to complement the gin, while the pickled bitter melon adds a salty, bittersweet bite to end the drink.

MAKES 1 DRINK
PREP TIME: 5 MINUTES

2 oz (60 ml) gin
1 oz (30 ml) dry vermouth
2 teaspoons brine from IPA-Pickled Bitter Melon
   (page 32)
Pickled bitter melon speared on a toothpick, for
   garnish

Combine the gin, vermouth and brine in a cocktail shaker filled with ice and stir vigorously (please don't shake) until well chilled, about 30 seconds. Strain into a chilled martini glass and garnish with the pickled bitter melon.

GIN POM COCKTAIL

Usually made with bottom-shelf gin and pomelo-flavored Tang, the Gin Pom is a popular cocktail in the Philippines for those seeking a buzz on the cheap. While I'm all for inexpensive imbibing, the standard Gin Pom could benefit from some tinkering.

Rather than using instant Tang, I take a cue from Snoop Dogg and add actual juice to my gin. In this case, it's fresh pomelo juice. Add a touch of Pandan Syrup to the mix and you've got yourself the best Gin Pom outside of Manila (and probably in Manila, too).

MAKES 1 DRINK
PREP TIME: 15 MINUTES

2 oz (60 ml) gin
1 oz (30 ml) fresh pomelo juice or grapefruit juice
(see "How to Peel a Pomelo" on page 63)
½ oz (15 ml) Pandan Syrup (page 45)
1 slice pomelo, for garnish

Combine the gin, pomelo juice, and Pandan Syrup in a cocktail shaker filled with ice and shake vigorously until well chilled, about 30 seconds. Strain into a chilled cocktail coupe and garnish with the pomelo slice.

RUM AND COCONUT WATER

Rum and coconut water: It's a simple, refreshing, centuries-old combination found in nearly any tropical climate that supports sugarcane, coconuts and perhaps pirates. Because they yield more sweet water than mature brown coconuts, a young green coconut (easily found at an Asian or Latin market) makes the ideal vessel for this drink. And yes, you can use store-bought coconut water in cans or tetra packs, but the pre-packaged stuff lacks the freshness, and fun, of drinking from a real coconut.

Any good rum will do in this recipe, but you don't want something that will overpower the nuanced sweetness and slight nuttiness of fresh coconut water. I find that golden rums, and even some aged rums, work well here. A squeeze of calamansi lime juice can lend some brightness as well, but isn't necessary if you'd rather not be bothered – this drink is meant to be relaxing, after all.

MAKES 1 DRINK
PREP TIME: 15 MINUTES

1 young green coconut (sometimes labeled
  as "Thai coconut"), refrigerated overnight
2 oz (60 ml) golden rum, such as Tanduay Gold
1 calamansi lime speared with a cocktail umbrella, for garnish

Carefully open the coconut as described on the facing page. Pour or sip out some of the coconut water to make room for the rum. Pour in the rum and garnish with the calamansi lime and cocktail umbrella. Serve immediately with a straw for sipping, as well as a spoon for scraping and eating a refreshing snack of fresh coconut meat after the drink is gone.

HOW TO OPEN A YOUNG COCONUT

Young green coconuts, sometimes called Thai coconuts, are easy to find at Asian and Latin markets. The young coconuts you'll find in the store will usually have their outer green shells already removed to expose a beige or light-brown inner husk; they are likely wrapped in plastic wrap.

In the Philippines, young green coconuts (known as *buko*) are expertly hacked open with machetes. While wielding a menacing machete can be an impressive spectacle for wide-eyed tourists, it isn't strictly necessary. All you need to open a young coconut at home is a sharp chef's knife or cleaver.

1. Firmly grasp the bottom of the coconut with your non-knife-holding hand, making sure to keep your fingers out of the way. Use the knife to carefully shave off the outer husk at the top of the coconut. Rotate the coconut and continue to shave around the top until the inner shell becomes exposed.
2. Strike the exposed inner shell of the coconut with the bottom corner of your knife until a crack or opening forms.
3. Wedge the blade of your knife into the opening and carefully lift your knife, using it as a lever.
4. The top part of the shell should easily come off in a single piece. Trim the exposed meat to widen the opening.

BARRELMAN BUCK

A buck cocktail, also known as a "mule," refers to any drink made with ginger beer, citrus juice, and a base spirit. This cocktail checks all those boxes, but perhaps more importantly, it's inspired by the infamous "Barrelman" souvenir from the Philippines. The Barrelman is a carving of a man wearing nothing but a barrel. (You might even say that he's "buck" naked.)

MAKES 1 DRINK
PREP TIME: 5 MINUTES

1 oz (30 ml) fresh calamansi juice or lime juice
1 oz (30 ml) bourbon whiskey
1 oz (30 ml) Filipino coconut liquor *(lambanog)*,
   or vodka
½ oz (15 ml) Lemongrass Honey Syrup (page 40)
3 dashes Angostura bitters
4 oz (120 ml) ginger beer, chilled
1 mint sprig, for garnish

Combine the calamansi juice, bourbon, *lambanog* or vodka, Lemongrass Honey Syrup, and bitters in a cocktail shaker filled with ice and shake vigorously until well chilled, about 30 seconds. Strain into a barrel Tiki mug or double old-fashioned glass filled with fresh ice cubes. Top off with chilled ginger beer and garnish with mint sprig.

LEMONGRASS HONEY SYRUP

Use this syrup to add light honey sweetness and a grassy citrus undertone to your cocktails.

MAKES ABOUT 1 CUP (250 ML)
PREP TIME: 5 MINUTES
COOK TIME: 15 MINUTES

1 stalk lemongrass, roughly chopped
½ cup (125 ml) water
½ cup (170 g) honey

Place the lemongrass and water in a small saucepan over medium heat. Bring to a boil, then cover saucepan, reduce heat to low and simmer for 5 minutes. Remove from the heat and allow the lemongrass to steep for 1 hour.

Place the honey in a small bowl and set aside.

Bring the lemongrass and water back to a boil. Remove from heat and pour the hot liquid through a fine-mesh strainer set over the bowl of honey. Discard the lemongrass. Stir the honey and lemongrass water together until the honey melts. Store in an airtight container for up to 2 weeks.

PANANTUKAN PUNCH

Known as "dirty boxing," *panantukan* refers to the striking aspects of Filipino martial arts – punching, elbows, knees, headbutts and the like – all used with the intent to overwhelm an opponent. Similarly, with a shot of Filipino coconut liquor hiding underneath a more flavorful and robust dark Jamaican rum, this punch packs a punch that you might not see coming.

MAKES 1 DRINK
PREP TIME: 5 MINUTES

1½ oz (45 ml) dark Jamaican rum
1 oz (30 ml) Filipino coconut liquor *(lambanog)* or vodka
1 oz (30 ml) fresh blood orange juice or fresh orange juice
1 oz (30 ml) mango juice
1 oz (30 ml) pineapple juice
½ oz (15 ml) Campari
Orange wheel, for garnish

Combine all of the cocktail ingredients except for the Campari in a cocktail shaker filled with ice and shake vigorously until well chilled, about 30 seconds. Strain into a tall Tiki mug or Collins glass filled with fresh ice cubes. Pour the Campari over the top of the cocktail and garnish with the orange wheel. Serve with a straw.

BARTENDER'S NOTE *Lambanog* is a Filipino spirit distilled from coconut tree sap. It's very similar to vodka in that it is fairly odorless and tasteless, despite its coconut origins. The Infanta brand of lambanog can be found at some Asian markets, and can be easily ordered online.

ISLAND HOPPER

This beer cocktail makes the most of the hoppy bitterness and tropical flavors of an IPA. The floral, piney notes in the gin sync with those in the beer, while the pineapple juice and grapefruit bitters echo the beer's citrus notes.

MAKES 1 DRINK
PREP TIME: 5 MINUTES

2 oz (60 ml) gin
2 oz (60 ml) pineapple juice
1 oz (30 ml) Lemongrass Honey Syrup (facing page)
2 dashes grapefruit bitters
3 oz (90 ml) American IPA, chilled
1 pineapple slice, for garnish

Combine the gin, pineapple juice, Lemongrass Honey Syrup and grapefruit bitters in a cocktail shaker filled with ice. Shake vigorously until well chilled, about 30 seconds. Strain into a large glass filled with ice, then slowly top off with the beer, waiting for the foam to subside as needed before filling the glass completely. Garnish with the pineapple slice and serve with a straw.

BRASS DONKEY

If you grew up in the '80s and '90s listening to rap music, you're probably familiar with the song "Brass Monkey," and the drink of the same name. Consisting of a 40-ounce bottle of malt liquor and some orange juice, the Brass Monkey drink was something I may have enjoyed once or twice during my college days, when malt liquor and rap music flowed more freely in my life. These days, it's more craft beer and nursery rhymes.

Because of my now advanced age (or perhaps in spite of it), I concocted the Brass Donkey: an upgrade on the Monkey but with a more manageable 16-ounce can of Filipino malt liquor, mango juice instead of orange juice, and some rum to make up for that lost 24 ounces of beer. While the Monkey was made for a solo drinker, the Donkey is a drink for two. And although there is no ice in this recipe, feel free to add some if you'd like, because Donkey "tastes def when you pour it on ice."

MAKES 2 DRINKS
PREP TIME: 5 MINUTES

One 16-oz (500-ml) can malt liquor, preferably
    San Miguel Red Horse, well chilled
12 oz (375 ml) mango juice, well chilled
2 oz (60 ml) silver rum (optional), such as
    Tanduay Silver
Quartered calamansi limes or lime wheels, for garnish

Divide the malt liquor, mango juice and rum equally between two tall glasses and stir. Garnish with limes and enjoy!

FROZEN CANTALOUPE AND CALAMANSI MARGARITA

Melon sa malamig (also known as melon drink, melon juice, or just *melón*) is a refreshing summertime cooler consisting of shredded cantaloupe mixed with water, sugar, and ice. This is my take on the classic Filipino drink, but in the form of a frosty blended margarita! I simply take a melon baller to the flesh of the cantaloupe, freeze the melon balls overnight, then blend them with ice-cold tequila and calamansi juice. What can I say? A cantaloupe, tequila and calamansi slushy might be more refreshing than the original melon sa malamig.

MAKES 2 DRINKS
PREP TIME: 15 MINUTES, PLUS 24 HOURS FOR FREEZING

1 small ripe cantaloupe, about 2.5 lbs (1 kg)
4 oz (120 ml) silver tequila
3 oz (90 ml) fresh calamansi juice or lime juice
1 oz (30 ml) agave syrup
¼ cup (35 g) coarse sea salt
1 calamansi lime cut in half, or 1 lime wedge

Rinse the cantaloupe well and cut it in half. Remove the seeds. Use a melon baller to scoop the cantaloupe flesh from each half. Place the melon balls in a single layer on a sheet pan or platter that will fit in your freezer. Freeze the melon balls overnight.

Combine the tequila and calamansi juice in a lidded container and store in the freezer overnight. The mixture will not freeze due to the alcohol in the tequila.

Place the frozen melon balls in a blender, along with the cold tequila and calamansi mixture. Add the agave syrup and pulse on high speed until completely smooth. Scrape down the sides of the blender as necessary. If you find the mixture to be too thick, you can thin it out with water, or more tequila, as needed.

Pour the salt onto a small plate. Rub the halved calamansi lime on the rims of two rocks or margarita glasses, then dip the rims into the salt. Divide the frozen margarita mixture between the two glasses and serve immediately.

MANGO MILKSHAKE MEMORY LANE

My wife and I once vacationed on Boracay, a small island in the Philippines known not only for its resorts and white sand beaches, but also for its famous fruit milkshakes. Wherever we went, there seemed to be a different restaurant, bar or snack shack with its own blended fruit and milk concoction. Our favorites were the Tart Green Mango Shake and Sweet Mango-Coconut Shake found at Jonah's, a beachside snack shack that specialized in fruit milkshakes. Our mango shakes were spiked with rum and served with a beautiful view, so it's no wonder we loved them so much. Whenever I long for another island getaway, I make these milkshakes!

TART GREEN MANGO SHAKE

Plain Greek yogurt adds creaminess to this shake and also provides a bit more tartness to go along with the tart green mango.

MAKES 1 DRINK
PREP TIME: 10 MINUTES

1 large unripe green mango (about 12 oz/350 g),
   peeled, pitted and roughly chopped
½ cup (100 g) ice
½ cup (125 ml) plain Greek yogurt
2 oz (60 ml) silver rum, such as Tanduay Silver
1 oz (30 ml) Pandan Syrup (facing page)
1 slice green mango, for garnish

Combine all of the ingredients in a blender and blend until smooth. Pour into a tall glass and garnish with the mango slice and cocktail umbrella. Serve with a straw.

SWEET MANGO COCONUT SHAKE

I prefer using store-bought frozen mango chunks in this shake, but you can use an equal quantity of fresh mangoes if you prefer. If you do so, just be sure to add a handful of ice to the blender.

MAKES 1 DRINK
PREP TIME: 5 MINUTES

8 oz (250 g) frozen mango chunks
1 cup (250 ml) coconut milk
1 oz (30 ml) Pandan Syrup (page 45)
2 oz (60 ml) golden rum, such as Tanduay Gold
1 calamansi lime for garnish

Combine the mango, coconut milk, syrup and rum in a blender and blend until smooth. Pour into a tall glass and garnish with the calamansi lime and a cocktail umbrella. Serve with a straw.

MIGUEL IN HELL

What happens when you cross a Mexican Michelada with everyone's favorite Filipino beer? You get the Miguel in Hell. With smoky mezcal, a fiery chili pepper, funky fish sauce and a rim kissed with tangy Filipino soup-mix powder, this drink will take your taste buds to hell and back – in a good way! Enjoy the ride.

MAKES 1 DRINK
PREP TIME: 10 MINUTES

1 tablespoon instant tamarind soup mix (see Bartender's Note)
1 calamansi lime half or lime wheel
1 Thai chili pepper, deseeded if less heat is desired
Heavy pinch of coarse sea salt
1 oz (30 ml) fresh calamansi juice or lime juice
2 teaspoons fish sauce
1 oz (30 ml) mezcal
One 12 oz (355 ml) bottle Filipino lager (San Miguel), chilled

Place the tamarind soup mix powder on a small plate. Rub the rim of a tall pint glass with the calamansi half or lime wheel and set the lime aside. Dip the rim of the glass into the tamarind soup mix powder. In the bottom of the pint glass, muddle together the chili pepper and salt. (Note: the more you muddle the pepper, the spicier the drink will be.)

Add the juice, fish sauce and mezcal and stir to combine. Fill the glass with ice, then top off with the lager. Garnish with the reserved lime and serve immediately.

BARTENDER'S NOTE Instant tamarind soup mix powder is usually used as a shortcut ingredient to make *sinigang*, a sour Filipino soup. Knorr, the most popular and readily available brand, can be easily found at Asian markets and in the Asian aisle of some neighborhood supermarkets.

PANDAN SYRUP

This syrup will add sweetness to cocktails, and impart a distinctive nutty aroma and flavor as well. Frozen pandan leaves can be easily found at Asian markets.

MAKES ABOUT 1 CUP (250 ML)
PREP TIME: 10 MINUTES
COOK TIME: 15 MINUTES

2 pandan leaves, thawed
1 cup (200 g) sugar
½ cup (125 ml) water

Rinse and dry the pandan leaves. Tie a knot in the middle of each leaf. Shred the leaves by inserting a fork into the leaf close to the knot and pulling the fork away from the knot.

Combine all ingredients in a small saucepan and bring to a boil over high heat, stirring until the sugar is dissolved. Lower heat and allow the mixture to simmer for 10 minutes, stirring occasionally. Remove from the heat and let the syrup come to room temperature. Remove and discard the leaves. Place the syrup in a sealed container and refrigerate for up to a month.

CHAPTER TWO

SMALL BITES
PICA-PICA & PINTXOS

Another word for pulutan is *pica-pica*, which roughly translates to "pick-pick." The recipes in this chapter range from small nibbles eaten out of hand, like peanuts and things on toast, to small mouthfuls and *pintxos* (items skewered on a toothpick), but they all epitomize "pick-pick" eating. One person could probably eat the output of an entire recipe on their own, but sharing is caring, right?

SPICY DEVILED EGGS WITH CRISPY BAGOONG BREADCRUMBS

The devil is in the details – especially in the case of these deviled eggs. With a creamy filling brightened by calamansi juice and spiced with fiery hot sauce, the eggs are given a final flourish with an umami-bomb topping of crunchy toasted breadcrumbs, garlic and fermented shrimp paste. You absolutely will not be able to eat just one.

SERVES 4 TO 6 AS AN APPETIZER
PREP TIME: 45 MINUTES
COOK TIME: 30 MINUTES

FOR THE EGGS:
6 eggs
2 tablespoons Garlic Bagoong Aioli (page 29) or store-bought mayonnaise
2 teaspoons fresh calamansi juice or lemon juice
1 to 2 teaspoons Green Mango Hot Sauce (page 28) or store-bought *sambal oelek* chili paste
Salt and pepper, to taste
Smoked paprika, for garnish

FOR THE TOPPING:
1 tablespoon olive oil
1 garlic clove, minced
1 teaspoon fermented shrimp paste (*bagoong*)
3 tablespoons panko breadcrumbs
1 tablespoon chopped fresh parsley
Salt and pepper, to taste

Prepare an ice bath in a large bowl. Set aside.

Cover the bottom of a large pot with 1 inch (2.5 cm) of water and place a steamer basket inside. Cover and place over high heat. When the water begins to boil, gently add the eggs to the steamer basket. Cover and steam for 13 minutes.

Transfer the eggs from the pot directly to the ice bath and let stand for 15 minutes. Carefully peel the eggs. Slice each egg in half lengthwise with a sharp knife.

Remove the yolks to a large bowl and set the egg whites aside on a separate platter. Mash the yolks with a fork until they are completely crumbled. Add the aioli, calamansi juice and hot sauce and stir until well combined. Add salt and pepper to taste.

Use a spatula or large spoon to transfer the yolk mixture to a small zip-top bag. Squeeze the mixture into one corner of the bag, then snip the corner off the bag with scissors. Gently squeeze the bag to pipe the filling into the cavity of each egg white. It's okay to overfill the eggs as necessary so that all of the yolk mixture is used. Sprinkle a pinch of smoked paprika over each egg and set aside.

To make the topping, heat the olive oil in a small nonstick pan over medium-high heat. When the oil begins to shimmer, add the garlic and shrimp paste and cook until the garlic just begins to brown, about 1 minute. Stir in the panko breadcrumbs and continue to cook until golden brown and crispy, about 2 minutes. Remove from heat and transfer the breadcrumb mixture to a medium bowl. Add the chopped parsley to the bowl and toss to combine. Season with salt and pepper to taste. Sprinkle the topping over the eggs and serve immediately.

UMINOM With its bready malt flavors, a German Helles beer syncs nicely with the toasted bread crumbs atop these deviled eggs, while still providing enough hop bitterness and effervescence to cut through the creamy and rich egg yolk filling. The lightness of the Helles is also a nice counterpoint to the funky shrimp paste in this dish.

Alternatively, for a contrast instead of a complement, Panantukan Punch (page 40) delivers a one-two punch of sweetness and high alcohol that will parry the salty, spicy kick of these deviled eggs very nicely.

SEA SALT AND VINEGAR PEANUTS MANI

Peanuts on their own are already a great bar snack. After a soak in Filipino vinegar and a sprinkling of Filipino sea salt, though, these peanuts go from average to addictive.

SERVES 4 TO 6 AS AN APPETIZER
PREP TIME: 5 MINUTES
COOK TIME: 15 MINUTES

¾ cup (185 ml) plus 1 tablespoon Filipino dark cane vinegar (*sukang iloco*) or apple cider vinegar, divided
1 lb (450 g) raw shelled peanuts
½ cup (125 ml) peanut or canola oil
Coarse sea salt, to taste
¼ teaspoon dried red pepper flakes
1 tablespoon chopped parsley

Combine the ¾ cup (185 ml) vinegar with the peanuts in a medium bowl. Let stand for 2 hours, stirring occasionally. Drain the peanuts, then spread them onto a sheet pan lined with paper towels to dry.

Heat the oil in a large cast-iron pan over moderately high heat until shimmering. Add half of the peanuts to the pan and cook, stirring, until golden, 3 to 5 minutes. Use a slotted spoon to transfer the peanuts to another sheet pan lined with paper towels. Season with sea salt. Repeat with the remaining peanuts.

Transfer the fried peanuts to a large bowl while they are still warm. Drizzle in the remaining tablespoon of vinegar, along with the red pepper flakes and the chopped parsley. Toss to combine. Season with additional sea salt and serve immediately.

UMINOM Don't overthink this. Versatile beers like Pilsners and pale ales deliver a great balance of malt and hops that won't overpower these peanuts. But if you must think, the citrus notes in a Saison will pucker up to the vinegar in these peanuts. Furthermore, a Saison's peppery bite is the perfect complement to the sea salt and helps to cut through the vinegar acidity.

AVOCADO TOAST WITH DRIED HIBE SHRIMP

Avocado toast is everywhere now. But so was shrimp toast 30 years ago. Every party my parents threw in the '80s involved smeared ground shrimp on Wonder bread. So I wonder if, 30 years from now, my kids will look back at avocado toast as some weird thing their dad made whenever he wanted a quick beer snack. It's very possible.

Until then, we have this avocado toast – avocados on Filipino *pan de sal* bread, spritzed with calamansi juice and bejeweled with tiny dried shrimp. Known as *hibe* in the Philippines, these small shrimp are usually used to add an umami boost to soups and stews, but here they add crunch and texture as well.

SERVES 4 TO 6 AS AN APPETIZER
PREP TIME: 10 MINUTES
COOK TIME: 5 MINUTES

3 mini Filipino pan de sal rolls, or Hawaiian
  sweet rolls, cut in half
1 clove garlic, peeled and cut in half
1 large avocado, pitted, peeled, and thinly sliced
Fresh calamansi juice or lime juice, to taste
Coarse sea salt, to taste
Freshly ground black pepper, to taste
Smoked paprika, to taste
Dried red pepper flakes, to taste
Small dried shrimp, to taste

Preheat the broiler on high. Place the rolls cut side up on a sheet pan. Toast directly under the broiler until golden brown, about 1 minute.

Rub the cut side of the garlic on each of the toasted rolls to infuse with garlic flavor. Lay an equal number of avocado slices on each toasted roll, spritz with calamansi juice, and season to taste with the spices. Place a few shrimp onto each roll, gently pressing them into the avocado so they stay put. Serve immediately.

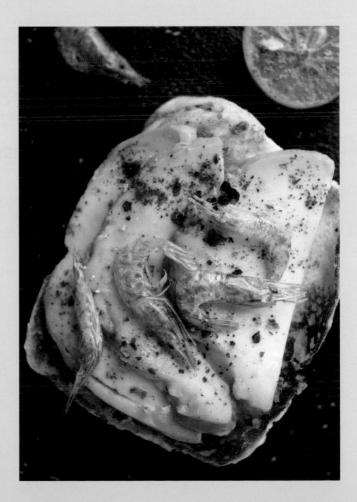

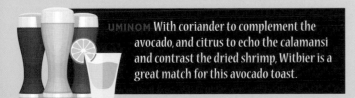

UMINOM With coriander to complement the avocado, and citrus to echo the calamansi and contrast the dried shrimp, Witbier is a great match for this avocado toast.

GRILLED TOMATO AND GREEN ONION SKEWERS ON TOAST
PAN DE SAL CON KAMATIS, BAGOONG, AT LASONA

Pan con tomate is a simple Catalonian tapas dish of fresh tomato grated onto a piece of toast. *Kamatis, bagoong, at lasona* is a simple Filipino condiment of tomatoes, fermented shrimp paste and shallots. Because I can't leave simple enough alone, I decided to blend these two seemingly separate items into one crowd-pleasing appetizer: grilled tomatoes are pressed onto toasted Filipino *pan de sal* bread, then drizzled with a dressing of olive oil, fermented shrimp paste and shallots.

SERVES 4 AS AN APPETIZER
PREP TIME: 30 MINUTES
COOK TIME: 10 MINUTES

1 tablespoon canola oil

2 teaspoons fermented shrimp paste (*bagoong*)

2 teaspoons Filipino dark cane vinegar (*sukang iloco*) or apple cider vinegar

1 tablespoon chopped shallots

1 lb (500 g) cherry tomatoes

3 green onions (scallions), cut into 1-in (2.5-cm) lengths

4 mini Filipino pan de sal rolls or Hawaiian sweet rolls, cut in half

Coarse sea salt and freshly ground black pepper, to taste

Six 12-in (30-cm) bamboo or metal skewers

If using bamboo skewers, soak them in water for at least 30 minutes prior to grilling. Preheat a grill for direct cooking.

Combine the canola oil, shrimp paste, vinegar and chopped shallots in a large bowl and whisk well to combine. Add the tomatoes and green onions to the bowl and toss to coat. Pour off the marinade and reserve.

Thread the tomatoes and green onions onto the skewers, alternating one tomato and two scallion segments, until there are 4 or 5 tomatoes on each skewer. Place skewers on the grill over direct high heat and grill, turning and rotating frequently, until the tomatoes and scallions are softened and charred, 3 to 4 minutes total. Remove the skewers from the grill and set aside to cool slightly.

Place the bread rolls cut side down on the hot side of the grill and toast until golden, about 1 minute. Transfer the toasted bread rolls to a platter, cut side up. Drizzle some of the reserved marinade onto the toast, then top with a few grilled tomatoes and green onions. Drizzle more of the reserved marinade over the tomatoes, then season with salt and pepper to taste. Serve immediately.

UMINOM Hefeweizen and tomatoes combine to deliver an incredible umami flavor on their own, but add bagoong to the mix and you've got an explosion of amazing savoriness.

COOK'S NOTE
Instead of serving the grilled tomatoes and green onions on bread, you can serve them as a condiment with grilled meats. After grilling, remove the tomatoes and green onions from the skewers and return them to the bowl with the reserved marinade. Smash a few of the tomatoes with a fork, then toss everything together to combine. Serve as a condiment alongside Grilled Pork Belly Skewers (page 106), Grilled Garlic Lamb Chops (page 105), or Beer-Marinated Chicken Skewers (page 104).

CORN-DOGGED QUAIL EGGS KWEK-KWEK

A popular street food in the Philippines, *kwek-kwek* are quail eggs that are hard-boiled, dipped in an orange-hued batter, deep-fried and then served on skewers. Sounds good, right? Well, they're even better when fried in a corn-dog batter.

SERVES 4 TO 6 AS AN APPETIZER
PREP TIME: 10 MINUTES
COOK TIME: 25 MINUTES

2 dozen quail eggs
½ cup (60 g) all-purpose flour
⅓ cup (50 g) cornmeal
2 teaspoons sugar
½ teaspoon salt, plus more to taste
½ teaspoon baking soda
1 large chicken egg, beaten
¼ to ½ cup (65 to 125 ml) beer,
    preferably a pale lager
Canola oil for frying

COOK'S NOTE Try covering Vienna sausages with this corn-dog batter to make mini corn dogs.

Prepare an ice bath in a large bowl. Set aside.

Gently place the quail eggs in a large saucepan and cover with cold water. Bring the saucepan to a boil over high heat, then continue to boil for 2 minutes. Remove the pan from heat, cover, and let stand for 2 minutes.

Remove the eggs from the saucepan and place them directly into the ice bath for 10 minutes. Carefully peel the eggs and set aside.

In a large bowl, whisk together the flour, cornmeal, sugar, salt and baking soda. Add the chicken egg and ¼ cup (65 ml) of the beer to the flour mixture, whisking until just combined. The mixture should resemble a thick cake batter. If it is too thick, add beer a tablespoon at a time as needed to thin it out.

Pour oil into a large pot or Dutch oven to reach a depth of 4 inches (10 cm). Heat the oil over high heat until it reaches 375°F (190°C) on a deep-fry thermometer. Alternatively, you can test the heat of the oil by dropping a small bit of batter into the oil. When it begins to immediately brown and sizzle, the oil is ready.

When the oil is ready, drop a few of the eggs into the batter. Using your fingers, turn the eggs until they are completely coated in the batter, then gently drop the battered eggs into the hot oil, working in batches as necessary. Fry, turning occasionally, until golden brown, 4 to 5 minutes. Adjust the heat as necessary to maintain the temperature of the oil. Transfer the corn-dogged eggs to a paper-towel-lined plate and season with salt. Serve with Green Mango Hot Sauce (page 28) or All-Purpose Vinegar Dip (page 31).

UMINOM Toasty, malty and nutty, Oktoberfest (or Märzen) beers deliver a slight caramel sweetness that resonates with the sweet corn batter of these quail eggs. Zippy hops deliver grease-cutting bitterness and offer a nice contrast to the rich egg yolks.

QUESO DE BOLA GRILLED CHEESE WITH JAM AND SHRIMP PASTE

Globes of Edam cheese covered in red wax are a common sight in the Philippines, where the cheese is known as *queso de bola* (meaning "ball of cheese"). Queso de bola is often grated onto Filipino desserts and pastries as a savory counterpoint.

Since queso de bola (or Edam) is such a great melting cheese, I like to use it alongside some pineapple jam and fermented fish paste for a singular sweet-and-salty grilled-cheese sandwich.

SERVES 2
PREP TIME: 10 MINUTES
COOK TIME: 10 MINUTES

4 tablespoons pineapple or mango jam

1 tablespoon chopped green onions (scallions)

1 to 2 teaspoons fermented shrimp paste (*bagoong*)

¼ teaspoon dried red pepper flakes

1 cup (80 g) shredded Edam or Gouda cheese

4 slices sandwich bread

4 tablespoons butter, divided

In a small bowl, mix together the jam, green onions, shrimp paste and red pepper flakes. Spread this mixture onto one side of all 4 slices of bread. Evenly distribute the cheese onto two slices of the bread, then top each cheese-topped slice of bread with the other slices, jammy sides facing inward.

Melt 2 tablespoons of the butter in a large cast-iron pan over medium heat, tilting the pan to swirl the butter around and coat the surface. Reduce the heat to medium-low and add the sandwiches. Cook, pressing with a metal spatula, until golden-brown on the first side, about 5 minutes. Transfer the sandwiches to a plate and melt the remaining 2 tablespoons butter in the pan. Return the sandwiches to the pan, browned-side up, and continue cooking until second side has browned and the cheese has melted, about 5 minutes more. Serve immediately.

UMINOM The roasted, nutty flavors in an American brown ale harmonize with the nuttiness of the cheese in this sandwich, while citrusy hops complement the jam and contrast the umami of the shrimp paste.

PORK MEATBALLS WITH SPICY COCONUT SAUCE BICOL EXPRESS

A rich and fragrant coconut sauce spiked with chilies, garlic and ginger will make these pork meatballs the star of your next get-together. Adjust the spice by varying the amount of chili peppers in the sauce.

SERVES 4 TO 6 AS AN APPETIZER
PREP TIME: 15 MINUTES
COOK TIME: 45 MINUTES

FOR THE MEATBALLS:

3 tablespoons coconut milk
2 tablespoons panko breadcrumbs
1 lb (500 g) ground pork
1-in (2.5-cm) piece fresh ginger, peeled and minced
1 tablespoon chopped green onions (scallions)
¼ teaspoon dried red pepper flakes
3 tablespoons coconut oil
¼ teaspoon coarse sea salt
¼ teaspoon freshly ground black pepper

FOR THE SAUCE:

1 tablespoon chopped shallots
2 cloves garlic, chopped
1-in (2.5-cm) piece fresh ginger, peeled and minced
1 or 2 Thai chili peppers, thinly sliced, plus more for garnish

1 teaspoon fermented shrimp paste (*bagoong*)
¼ cup (65 ml) white wine
¾ cup (185 ml) coconut milk
1 tablespoon fish sauce
1 tablespoon fresh calamansi juice or lemon juice, plus more to taste
2 teaspoons brown sugar, plus more to taste
Salt and freshly ground black pepper, to taste

Make the meatballs: Combine the 3 tablespoons coconut milk with the panko breadcrumbs in a large bowl and let sit for 5 minutes. Add the ground pork, ginger, green onions, dried red pepper flakes, salt and pepper. Mix with a rubber spatula until just combined. Do not overwork the meat mixture. Form meatballs about 1 inch (2.5 cm) in diameter by rolling about 1 tablespoon of the meat mixture between your palms. Place the formed meatballs on a large platter.

Heat the oil in a large sauté pan over medium heat. Working in batches if necessary, add the meatballs to the pan. Cook, turning occasionally, until the meatballs are browned on all sides but not yet cooked through, about 10 minutes per batch. Transfer the browned meatballs to a large platter and set aside.

Make the sauce: Add the shallots, garlic, ginger, chili peppers and shrimp paste to the hot pan and cook, stirring, until the shallots soften and begin to turn translucent, 2 to 3 minutes. Pour the wine into the hot pan, stirring to scrape up any browned bits from the bottom. Increase the heat to high and whisk in the ¾ cup (185 ml) coconut milk, fish sauce, calamansi juice and brown sugar. Return the meatballs to the pan, bring the liquid to a boil, then reduce heat to low. Cover the pan and simmer the meatballs until cooked through, about 5 minutes. Taste the sauce and add more juice, sugar, salt and pepper as needed.

Garnish with sliced chili peppers, and serve with cocktail picks or forks.

UMINOM The citrusy hops in American pale ales harmonize with the calamansi in the sauce, while providing enough bitterness to cut through the coconut milk and lift the chili spice.

SAUTÉED MUSHROOMS WITH LEMONGRASS

These tapas-style mushrooms get some Filipino punches of flavor with lemongrass, dark cane vinegar, and fish sauce. They're also easy to prepare and can be made ahead of time and reheated without anyone being the wiser.

SERVES 4 TO 6
PREP TIME: 10 MINUTES
COOK TIME: 15 MINUTES

2 tablespoon olive oil, plus more for serving
1 stalk lemongrass, bottom 4 to 6 in (10 to 15 cm) trimmed and finely minced
4 cloves garlic, minced
¼ teaspoon dried red pepper flakes, plus more to taste
1 lb (500 g) white button mushrooms, cleaned and quartered
Pinch of coarse sea salt, plus more to taste
1 tablespoon Filipino dark cane vinegar (*Sukang Iloco*), or apple cider vinegar
1 tablespoon fish sauce
Freshly ground black pepper, to taste
1 tablespoon roughly chopped parsley

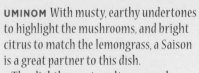

UMINOM With musty, earthy undertones to highlight the mushrooms, and bright citrus to match the lemongrass, a Saison is a great partner to this dish.

The slightly sweet, malty, caramel flavors of a German Dunkel complement and emphasize the rich umami flavors in the mushrooms and fish sauce, while the beer also has earthy undertones to accentuate the mushrooms as well.

Heat the oil in a large sauté pan over moderately high heat. Add the lemongrass, garlic, and red pepper flakes and cook until the garlic just begins to brown, 2–3 minutes. Add the mushrooms and a pinch of salt and cook, stirring occasionally, until the mushrooms become tender and begin to release some liquid, 2–3 minutes.

Stir in the vinegar and fish sauce and continue cooking until most of the liquid has been reabsorbed into the mushrooms, 2–3 minutes. Taste the mushrooms and season with salt and pepper as needed. Transfer the mushrooms to a serving dish, drizzle on more olive oil, sprinkle on parsley and more red pepper flakes if desired. Serve with cocktail forks or toothpicks.

CHAPTER THREE

THE RAW AND THE (BARELY) COOKED

Minimal heat, minimal flame and minimal cooking – or in some instances, no cooking at all – are needed for the recipes in this section. From just-shucked oysters and raw fish to salad-filled crepes and barely cooked shrimp, freshness is the key to these Filipino dishes.

FILIPINO SALAD CREPES LUMPIANG SARIWA

Not all *lumpia* are created crispy. *Lumpiang sariwa*, also known as "fresh lumpia," are crepes filled with raw vegetables and served cold – a lighter, fresher alternative to the hot, crunchy, deep-fried variety of Filipino spring roll.

Packed with a simple slaw of cabbage and carrots dressed in a pungent peanut sauce, the lumpia here are wrapped in a crepe made with beer and coconut milk. Though it's not traditional, I like to top these salad-filled crepes with a fried egg, which adds a nice contrast in temperature, not to mention a rich egg yolk to mingle with the peanut sauce.

MAKES 4 TO 6 SERVINGS
PREP TIME: 20 MINUTES
COOK TIME: 20 MINUTES

FOR THE CREPES:
2 eggs
½ cup (125 ml) coconut milk
½ cup (125 ml) beer, preferably a light lager
1 tablespoon melted coconut oil, plus more for pan
¾ cup (90 g) all-purpose flour

FOR THE DRESSING:
2 tablespoons fresh calamansi juice or lime juice
2 tablespoons fish sauce
2 tablespoons sugar
2 tablespoons all-natural smooth peanut butter
¼ teaspoon red pepper flakes

FOR THE FILLING:
2 cups shredded red cabbage
2 cups shredded savoy cabbage
1 carrot, peeled and grated
1 green onion (scallion), thinly sliced
1 tablespoon chopped cilantro
1 tablespoon chopped peanuts

OPTIONAL TOPPING:
6 fried eggs (one for each crepe)

UMINOM American amber lagers, with their toasty caramel sweetness, lift up and accentuate the sweet peanut sauce in this dish. The beer's spicy floral notes complement the red pepper flakes and green onions, while a moderate hop bitterness helps to contrast the salty fish sauce.

The Miguel in Hell beer cocktail (page 45) is a great spicy accompaniment to these crepes – especially if they're served topped with fried eggs.

To make the crepes, whisk together the eggs, coconut milk, beer and melted coconut oil in a large bowl. Add the flour to the bowl a third at a time, completely whisking in each addition before adding the next. Let the batter sit at room temperature for 1 hour.

To make the dressing, combine all dressing ingredients in a small bowl and whisk until well combined. Set aside until ready to serve.

To make the filling, combine all filling ingredients in a large bowl and toss until well combined. Place in the refrigerator until ready to serve.

When you are ready to cook the crepes, heat a 10-inch (25-cm) nonstick skillet over medium heat. Brush the skillet with a thin film of coconut oil, then pour about ⅓ cup (100 ml) of the batter into the hot skillet, rotating the skillet so that the batter evenly coats the bottom in a thin layer. Cook the first side of the crepe until golden brown, 1 to 2 minutes. Gently flip the crepe over and cook the other side for 30 seconds. Transfer the cooked crepe to a large plate and cover it with foil to keep it warm. Repeat until all of the batter is used. If you will be topping the crepes with fried eggs, you can use the same skillet to fry six eggs.

To serve, pour the dressing over the salad and toss well. Place a mound of the dressed salad in the center of a crepe. Top with a fried egg if desired, then roll or fold the crepe. Repeat until all the crepes are filled. Serve immediately.

TOFU AND CAVIAR WITH FISH SAUCE AND CALAMANSI CARAMEL

Sold by Filipino street vendors, *taho* is a sweet snack that usually features silken tofu and chewy tapioca pearls drizzled with sweet caramel sauce. My savory twist on the dessert has briny roe instead of tapioca, and Fish Sauce and Calamansi Caramel replacing the usual brown sugar syrup.

MAKES 3 TO 6 SERVINGS
PREP TIME: 5 MINUTES
COOK TIME: 20 MINUTES (TO MAKE THE CARAMEL)

12 oz (350 g) firm tofu
1 recipe Fish Sauce and Calamansi Caramel (page 27)
Freshly ground black pepper, to taste
1 tablespoon chopped chives
Salmon roe caviar, to taste

Drain the tofu and pat dry. Cut into six equal cubes and place each cube in a small serving dish. Drizzle some of the Fish-Sauce Caramel onto each cube of tofu, season with black pepper, garnish with chopped chives and top with as much or as little salmon roe caviar as desired.

UMINOM Crisp, clean and refreshing, a German Pilsner delivers on multiple fronts to match this tofu dish. Floral aromatics harmonize with the calamansi in the caramel, while a slight malt sweetness marries with the sweetness of the caramel. The beer's palate-cleansing bitterness and bubbly effervescence provides a contrast to the salty salmon roe and umami-rich fish sauce.

GIN, POMELO AND SHRIMP COCKTAIL KINILAW NA HIPON

I found inspiration for this *kinilaw*-style shrimp cocktail in the classic Gin-Pom Cocktail (drinking a few Gin-Poms will put some ideas in your head, I suppose). With spicy ginger and chili peppers and the bright acid of fresh calamansi juice, this dish has all the hallmarks of a classic kinilaw. Its barely cooked shrimp serve as a perfect alternative for those averse to raw fish.

The pomelo delivers bursts of juicy sweetness to complement the plump shrimp, while a splash of gin adds a nice boozy undertone for all the citrus. While any high-quality gin will do in this recipe, I prefer Hendrick's brand, as its cucumber notes go particularly well with the fresh cucumber in this dish.

MAKES 4 TO 6 SERVINGS
PREP TIME: 15 MINUTES
COOK TIME: 10 MINUTES

1 lb (500 g) large shrimp, peeled and deveined
6 or 7 peeled pomelo segments broken into bite-sized pieces, or grapefruit segments cut into bite-sized pieces
1 Thai bird chili pepper, thinly sliced
1 jalapeño chili pepper, seeded and diced
½ cup diced cucumber
1 shallot, minced
1-in (2.5-cm) piece fresh ginger, peeled and grated
4 or 5 fresh mint leaves, roughly torn
1 oz (30 ml) gin
3 oz (90 ml) fresh calamansi juice or lime juice
Coarse sea salt and freshly ground pepper, to taste
Fresh calamansi limes, halved, or regular lime wedges, for serving

UMINOM The Gin-Pom Cocktail (page 37) is a natural match for this gin-pom kinilaw.

California Common beers, also known as steam beers, feature faint minty hop aromas and flavors that form a nice bridge to the mint in this dish. A light fruitiness in the beer complements the pomelo, while a bracing bitterness provides contrast to the sourness of the calamansi. A crisp rosé wine would also be great with these shrimp.

Prepare an ice bath in a large bowl. Set aside.

Bring 3 quarts (2.5 liters) of water to a boil in a large pot set over high heat. Once the water comes to a boil, remove from the heat and immediately place the shrimp in the pot. Stir until the shrimp turn bright pink, their tails curl and they are just cooked through, 1 to 2 minutes total.

Use a slotted spoon or spider strainer to remove the shrimp from the hot water and transfer them to the prepared ice bath. When completely cool, strain and dry the shrimp, then cut them into ¼-inch (6-mm) pieces. Place in a large bowl and set in the refrigerator until ready to serve.

When ready to serve, add the pomelo, chili peppers, cucumber, shallot, ginger, mint, gin and calamansi juice to the shrimp in the large bowl. Use a rubber spatula or large spoon to gently stir the ingredients together, then add salt and pepper to taste.

Serve immediately with fresh calamansi halves or lime wedges for squeezing over the kinilaw.

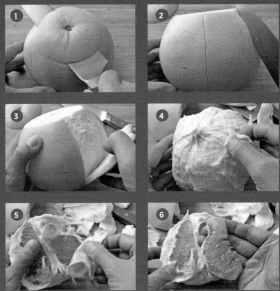

HOW TO PEEL A POMELO

Although it looks similar to a grapefruit, a pomelo takes a bit more effort to peel due to its thick rind and pith. A tough membrane between each segment of pomelo allows the segments to keep their shape quite well after being peeled.

1. Use a sharp knife to slice off the very top of the pomelo rind.
2. Make two vertical slits in the rind from top to bottom of the pomelo, about 2 inches (5 cm) apart. Cut through the rind and pith without cutting into the fruit within.
3. With your fingers, peel away the first section of rind between the two slits cut in the previous step. Then peel away the rest of the thick rind from the pomelo.
4. Peel away as much white pith as you can from the exterior of the pomelo, then pull the fruit apart from the center so that it is in two halves.
5. Working with the first pomelo half, remove the thick membrane between each citrus segment.
6. Carefully remove the segments of pomelo. Each one should easily come off in one piece.
   Continue until all pomelo segments are peeled and free of any thick membrane or white pith. At this point you can break the segments into bite-sized pieces by hand or slice them with a knife.

RAW YELLOWTAIL WITH CALAMANSI AND VINEGAR KINILAW NA ISDA

Kinilaw is an indigenous Filipino dish of incredible freshness, usually (but not always) featuring morsels of raw seafood quickly bathed in native vinegar, citrus, or both, and then garnished with any number of sinus-clearing, palate-awakening aromatics and spices including ginger, green onions and chilies.

 Although kinilaw can be served with the fish already dressed in the aforementioned fixings, I've come to prefer preparing the fish with minimal ingredients, and leaving the rest up to my guests with a vinegar dipping sauce and calamansi limes on the side. Kinilaw customization is king. This recipe can easily be doubled.

MAKES 2 TO 4 SERVINGS
PREP TIME: 15 MINUTES

1 lb (500 g) yellowtail, cut into ½-in (1.25-cm) cubes
1-in (2.5 cm) piece fresh ginger, peeled and grated
1 teaspoon lemon zest
1 teaspoon lime zest
1 small lemon, sliced very thin
1 lime, sliced very thin
Coarse sea salt, to taste
1 green onion (scallion) sliced very thin
12 calamansi limes, cut in half
1 recipe All-Purpose Vinegar Dip (page 31)
2 or 3 Thai chili peppers, thinly sliced (optional)

In a large bowl, gently toss together the fish, ginger, lemon zest and lime zest. Cover and refrigerate until ready to serve.

 To serve, arrange the lemon and lime slices in layers on a cutting board or serving dish. Pile the prepared fish cubes on top of the citrus slices. Sprinkle with salt to season and garnish with green onions.

 Serve the fish with the calamansi halves and All-Purpose Vinegar Dip alongside as condiments and cocktail picks for spearing. Add the sliced chili peppers to the vinegar dip if you like it spicy, or serve them on the side.

COOK'S NOTE
Because freshness is key to any kinilaw, use whatever sashimi-grade fish is local to you.

UMINOM The bright acidity of a tart Gueuze (pronounced "ger-zuh") goes well with this kinilaw.
 For something more approachable, think Mexican-style lagers, or perhaps more appropriately, Filipino-style lagers.

RAW OYSTERS WITH GREEN MANGO AND CALAMANSI KINILAW NA TALABA

Paho, a species of small and sour green mango found in the Philippines, are often used to add texture and tartness to raw fish preparations. Although not as tart as their diminutive cousins, unripe common green mangoes are more widely available, and add a sour crunch of their own that goes great with raw, briny oysters.

The *kinilaw* preparation below is strictly DIY for you and your guests, and it happens to be my favorite way to make it. Customize your own oyster with whatever amount of green mango, spices, and citrus juice you desire. Note: To shuck the oysters, see page 18.

MAKES 2 TO 4 SERVINGS
PREP TIME: 20 MINUTES

1 tablespoon finely diced unripe green mango
1 tablespoon dried red pepper flakes
1 tablespoon coarse sea salt
1 tablespoon freshly ground black pepper
One dozen fresh live oysters, cleaned and shucked
Calamansi limes or lemon wedges, for squeezing

Place each seasoning – green mango, red pepper flakes, salt and black pepper – in a separate serving dish.

According to individual taste, add as much or as little of each seasoning to each oyster as desired. Squeeze the calamansi or lemon over, then slurp and enjoy.

UMINOM Just as with the yellowtail kinilaw on the facing page, a tart Gueuze is a nearly perfect accompaniment to these oysters. Its moderate acidity harmonizes with the calamansi juice and green mangoes while also providing a nice contrast to the oyster's saltiness. Although sour and complex, a Gueuze will highlight oysters and not overpower them.

A classic wine pairing with oysters is Muscadet. With a mildly saline, mineral-like quality, flanked by citrus and floral notes, this crisp wine echoes all the notes of briny oysters spritzed with citrus juice.

CHAPTER FOUR

FRIED, SIZZLED & SEARED

Fact: Food tastes better when it's cooked in hot fat. Nowhere is this more apparent than in the array of delicious Filipino finger foods that emerge from a hot frying pan. Crispy spring rolls, spicy hot wings, sizzling squid – the dishes in this chapter are sublime on their own, and even better when paired with a cold beer.

FRIED GREEN MANGOES

Essentially the Filipino equivalent to salt-and-vinegar potato chips, green mango with a smear of *bagoong* fermented shrimp paste is a popular snack in the Philippines, combining the tartness of an unripe mango with the salty umami of the bagoong.

While a crisp wedge of raw green mango dabbed in bagoong is indeed delicious, I've found that green mangoes can be just as tasty fried. After frying, their natural sweetness becomes more pronounced, making for a sweet-and-sour mango encased in a crispy crust.

These golden-crusted green mangoes are still great when dipped in bagoong, but they're even better when dipped in Garlic Bagoong Aioli or Green Mango Hot Sauce.

MAKES 4 TO 6 SERVINGS
PREP TIME: 20 MINUTES
COOK TIME: 20 MINUTES

½ cup (25 g) panko bread crumbs
½ cup (70 g) cornmeal
¼ teaspoon freshly ground black pepper
½ cup (80 g) rice flour
1 egg, beaten
½ cup (125 ml) milk
2 large green mangoes, peeled, pitted and cut into ½ in (1.25 cm) thick wedges
Canola oil, for frying
Salt, to taste

In a large, shallow dish, combine the panko, cornmeal and pepper. Stir to blend and set aside. Place the rice flour in another shallow dish. Whisk together the egg and milk in a third shallow dish.

Dredge the mango wedges in the rice flour, shaking off any excess, then dip in the egg mixture. Finally, roll in the panko mixture to coat. Set the breaded mango wedges on a wire rack until ready to fry.

Pour oil into a large frying pan or deep skillet to reach a depth of 1 inch (2.5 cm). Heat the oil over high heat until it reaches 375°F (190°C) on a deep-fry thermometer. Working in batches, fry the mango until golden brown and crispy, 2 to 3 minutes per side. Be sure to adjust the heat as necessary to maintain the oil temperature. Drain the fried mango wedges on a paper-towel-lined plate and season with salt, to taste.

Serve with Garlic Bagoong Aioli (page 29) or Green Mango Hot Sauce (page 28).

UMINOM Frying sweetens the green mangoes just enough to balance out their tartness. A Belgian Tripel offers a slight honey-like sweetness to match the natural sugars in the fruit and to contrast the green mango's sourness. Spicy and peppery hops complement the fried crust, while notes of citrus and funk form a natural bridge to the aioli dipping sauce.

FRIED CALAMARI WITH CRISPY PURPLE YAM CRUST

A coating of Filipino purple yam *(ube)* flour adds a slight purple tinge to the calamari while also providing a crisp, cornmeal-like texture after emerging from the hot oil.

MAKES 4 SERVINGS
PREP TIME: 25 MINUTES
COOK TIME: 15 MINUTES

Canola oil, for frying
1 lb (500 g) cleaned fresh squid, tubes and tentacles
½ cup (60 g) all-purpose flour
½ cup (80 g) purple yam (ube) flour or cornmeal
½ teaspoon cayenne pepper
¼ teaspoon freshly ground black pepper
Coarse sea salt, to taste
1 tablespoon chopped parsley, for garnish
Lemon wedges or halved calamansi limes, for squeezing

In a large pot or Dutch oven, pour in enough oil to reach a depth of 4 inches (10 cm). Heat the oil over high heat until it reaches 375°F (190°C) on a deep-fry thermometer.

While the oil heats, rinse the squid under cold water and drain well. Cut the tubes into ½-inch (1.25 cm) rings, and cut any large sets of tentacles in half lengthwise. Set squid aside.

In a large bowl, whisk together the flours, cayenne and black pepper. Working in batches, add a handful of the squid to the bowl and dredge until well coated.

Transfer the coated squid to a large mesh strainer set over the flour mixture. Shake off any excess dredge from the squid. Place the coated squid into the hot oil and fry until golden, 1 to 2 minutes. Transfer the fried calamari to a large plate lined with paper towels and season with salt. Repeat until all squid is fried, adjusting the heat as necessary to maintain the oil temperature.

Garnish calamari with parsley. Serve immediately with lemon or calamansi limes, along with Garlic Bagoong Aioli (page 29) or Green Mango Hot Sauce (page 28).

UMINOM Hoppy German and American Pilsners, as well as Brut Champagne, all match well with these calamari.

CHICKEN-FRIED EGGPLANT TORTANG TALONG

The term *tortang talong*, which translates to "eggplant omelet," refers to a dish in which charred eggplant are dipped in beaten eggs and then fried. In this chicken-fried version, I give the eggplant a good dredge in seasoned flour before dipping it in the beaten egg. The result features a crisp and flavorful exterior shell to complement the smoky eggplant within.

MAKES 3 TO 4 SERVINGS
PREP TIME: 15 MINUTES
COOK TIME: 25 MINUTES

3 medium Asian eggplants,
  7 to 10 in (18 to 25 cm) each
½ cup (60 g) all-purpose flour
½ teaspoon sweet paprika
¼ teaspoon salt, plus more to taste
¼ teaspoon freshly ground black pepper
¼ teaspoon garlic powder
⅛ teaspoon ground red pepper (cayenne)
2 eggs
Canola oil, for frying

UMINOM The rich, malty flavor of a German Altbier or American brown ale resonates with the smoky eggplant flavor and crisp coating. These beers also provide enough hop bitterness and carbonation to cut through the oiliness of fried food.

Pierce the eggplants all over with the tip of a sharp knife and cover the stem ends with foil. Place eggplants on a sheet pan directly under the broiler and broil, turning over once, until the skin is charred all over and the eggplant is soft, 10 to 15 minutes total. Set aside to cool.

Combine the flour, paprika, salt, pepper, garlic powder and cayenne in a shallow dish and whisk well. Break the eggs into a separate shallow dish, beat well and set next to the flour mixture.

Discard the foil on the eggplant stems. Peel and discard the charred skin from the eggplants, leaving the stems intact.

Gently press each eggplant with a fork to form steaks about ¼ inch (6 mm) thick.

Holding one eggplant by the intact stem, dredge in the flour mixture and shake off the excess flour. Dip in the beaten eggs, then dredge in the flour mixture again. Set aside on a wire rack until ready to fry. Repeat with remaining eggplants.

Pour enough oil into a large frying pan or deep skillet to reach a depth of 1 inch (2.5 cm). Heat the oil over high heat until it reaches 375°F (190°C) on a deep-fry thermometer. Working in batches, fry the eggplant until golden brown and crispy, 2–3 minutes per side. Adjust the heat as necessary to maintain the oil temperature.

Drain the fried eggplant on a paper towel-lined plate and season with salt. Serve with ketchup, sriracha or Green Mango Hot Sauce (page 28).

PIGS' EAR AND TOFU SPRING ROLLS LUMPIANG TOKWA'T BABOY

Tokwa't baboy is a Filipino dish consisting of boiled pigs' ears and fried tofu served with a sweet and salty soy-based sauce. I've essentially distilled that dish down and stuffed it into a *lumpia* fried spring roll. Why? Because for me, the original tokwa't baboy always seemed to be lacking in texture. With a lumpia version, you get the crispness of the fried spring roll shell offsetting the tender pigs' ears and soft tofu. And I didn't forget about the sauce – just dip these delights in Sweet and Sharp Shallot Sauce.

MAKES 4 TO 6 SERVINGS (24 SPRING ROLLS)
PREP TIME: 30 MINUTES
COOK TIME: 4 HOURS, 10 MINUTES

FOR THE PIGS' EARS:

1 lb (500 g) cleaned pigs' ears
   (about 2 ears)
1 carrot, roughly chopped
1 onion, roughly chopped
2 stalks celery, roughly chopped
3 cloves garlic, smashed and peeled
1 teaspoon whole black peppercorns
1 bay leaf

FOR THE SPRING ROLLS:

8 oz (250 g) firm tofu, diced small
1 small carrot, grated
4 tablespoons chopped cilantro
2 tablespoons chopped green onions
   (scallions)
½ teaspoon coarse sea salt
¼ teaspoon freshly ground black
   pepper
25 square spring roll wrappers (8 x 8
   in/20 x 20 cm), thawed if frozen
Canola oil, for frying

Place the pigs' ears into a large pot or Dutch oven and add enough cold water to cover by at least 2 inches (5 cm). Place the pot over high heat, bring to a boil and continue boiling for 5 minutes. Drain the ears in a large colander set in the sink and rinse with cold running water. Rinse out the pot as well.

Return the ears to the cleaned pot, then add the carrots, onions, celery, garlic, peppercorns and bay leaf. Add enough cold water to cover everything by at least 2 inches (5 cm). Bring the pot to a boil over high heat, then reduce heat to low and simmer for 3 to 4 hours, until the ears can be easily pierced with a fork. Transfer the ears to a plate and allow to cool. You can strain and freeze the stock for another use if desired.

At this point, the prepared pigs' ears may be stored in the refrigerator up to a day in advance if needed.

When you are ready to make the lumpia, chop the pigs' ears into small pieces and place in a large bowl. Add the tofu, grated carrot, cilantro, green onions, salt and pepper and toss well to combine. Use this mixture to fill and roll the lumpia according to the steps on the facing page. They may be frozen at this point for future use.

To fry the lumpia, pour cooking oil into a large frying pan to a depth of at least 1 inch (2.5 cm). Heat the oil over high heat until it reaches 375°F (190°C) on a deep-fry thermometer. Working in batches, fry the lumpia, turning occasionally, until golden brown and crisp, 3 to 5 minutes total. (If frying frozen lumpia, add an extra 1 to 2 minutes). Transfer the fried lumpia to a paper-towel-lined plate and serve immediately with Sweet and Sharp Shallot Sauce (page 30).

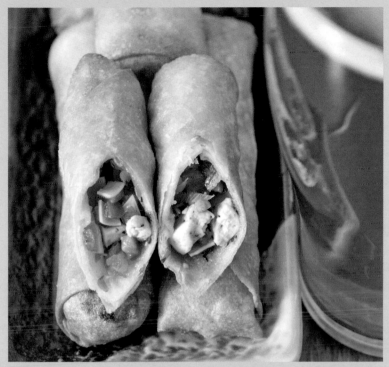

HOW TO ROLL LUMPIA:

1. Place 1 spring roll wrapper on a clean, dry work surface so that one corner of the wrapper is pointing at you (i.e., positioned like a diamond rather than a square). Place 1 heaping tablespoon of the filling just under the midpoint of the diamond, closest to the corner pointing at you.
2. Take the corner closest to you and roll it up and over the filling until half of the wrapper remains
3. Fold the left and right corners of the wrapper over the filling.
4. Using your fingers or a pastry brush, dab the edges of the wrapper with water, and then continue to roll the lumpia toward the final corner at the top.

Set the rolled lumpia aside underneath a moist towel, and continue rolling until all of the filling has been used.

To freeze the lumpia, arrange them in a single layer on a baking sheet and place in the freezer until completely frozen. Transfer the frozen lumpia to a large resealable food storage bag and store in the freezer for up to 3 months.

UMINOM Fried lumpia are almost always served with a vinegar-based dipping sauce that has a sharp acidic bite to cut through the fat of the frying oil. A sour beer like a tart Berliner Weiss will have a similarly pleasing effect when paired with these rolls.

The citrus and pine notes in an American pale ale are a nice bridge to the cilantro in these spring rolls, while the slight hop bitterness and carbonation will cut through the richness of the fried lumpia shell and pigs' ears.

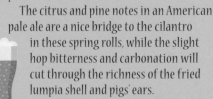

WOK-BLISTERED SHISHITO PEPPERS

Quickly charred in a blazing-hot wok, then showered with calamansi lime juice and Filipino sea salt, these crunchy blistered *shishito* peppers are as addictive a bar snack as they are easy to prepare. And although it's said that one in every ten shishito peppers packs a spicy and pungent punch, those are some low-risk/high-reward stakes, if you ask me. Besides, if you do end up pulling an especially spicy pepper, a cold beer or cocktail always makes everything better. If you can't find shishito peppers, you can use padrón peppers or Italian frying peppers instead.

MAKES 4 SERVINGS
PREP TIME: 5 MINUTES
COOK TIME: 5 MINUTES

1 lb (500 g) whole shishito peppers
1 tablespoon canola oil
Calamansi limes, for squeezing
Coarse sea salt, to taste

In a large bowl, toss together the peppers and oil until all the peppers are evenly coated.

Heat a large flat-bottomed wok or large cast-iron skillet over high heat until smoking. Add half of the peppers to the wok in a single layer and cook, undisturbed, for 1 minute. Toss and stir-fry the peppers for another 2 to 3 minutes until blistered all over. Transfer to a serving dish. Repeat with the remaining peppers.

Spritz the peppers with calamansi juice and sprinkle with sea salt to taste. Serve immediately.

UMINOM Hop bitterness tends to intensify spicy heat on the palate. But if you're the masochistic type, a West Coast–style IPA with citrus and tropical fruit notes would do well with these slightly fruity sweet peppers.

The lemon and pepper notes in a Saison would complement the citrus of the calamansi and the inherent spice in the peppers without intensifying them too much.

The carbonation, malt sweetness and mango in the Brass Donkey cocktail (page 42) would combine to make a great foil for these spicy, salty, citrusy peppers, too.

COOK'S NOTE To blister shishito peppers on the grill, thread the peppers onto skewers, brush with the oil, and place on a grill over direct high heat. Grill for 2 to 3 minutes per side until charred and blistered all over. Spritz the blistered peppers with calamansi juice and sprinkle with sea salt to taste. Serve immediately.

CRISPY FRIED SMELT DILIS

Smelt can be found at Asian markets and specialty seafood stores, but any small fish of similar size can be substituted. Diminutive smelt can be eaten whole – bones, guts and all – which makes them ideal for frying.

The rice-flour coating on these smelt gives them a nice, light crispness. They're the best French fries with eyes you'll ever eat – and they pair wonderfully with a cold beer.

MAKES 4 TO 6 SERVINGS
PREP TIME: 5 MINUTES
COOK TIME: 15 MINUTES

1 cup (150 g) rice flour
½ teaspoon sweet paprika
½ teaspoon garlic powder
½ teaspoon freshly ground black pepper
Canola oil, for frying
1 lb (500 g) fresh smelt
Coarse sea salt, to taste
1 tablespoon chopped chives, for garnish

Stir together the rice flour, paprika, garlic powder and black pepper in a shallow dish and set aside.

Pour oil into a large frying pan to a depth of at least 1 inch (2.5 cm). Heat the oil over high heat until it reaches 375°F (190°C) on a deep-fry thermometer.

As the oil heats, dredge the smelt in the flour mixture until evenly coated. Place the coated smelt on a wire rack set over a sheet pan.

Working in batches, fry the smelt, turning occasionally, until golden blonde and crisp, 5 to 6 minutes. Transfer to a paper-towel-lined plate and season with salt, to taste. Repeat, adjusting the heat as necessary to maintain the temperature. Garnish with the chopped chives.

Serve fried smelt with All-Purpose Vinegar Dip (page 31) or Spicy Fish Sauce and Calamansi Dip (page 26).

UMINOM This dish is essentially a Filipinized version of English fish and chips. As such, English pale ale or extra-special bitter (ESB) pairs well. The biscuity malts in the beer echo the crispy coating, while the bitterness cuts the fat and contrasts the vinegar.

SPICY SIZZLING SQUID SISIG NA PUSIT

Sisig, in its original porky form of chopped pigs' ears and snout served on a sizzling platter, has become quite popular in the US. This is thanks in large part to the likes of Anthony Bourdain singing its praises, not to mention the enterprising Filipino-American cooks serving sisig everywhere from food trucks (ahem, #humblebrag) to brick-and-mortar restaurants.

If you travel to the Philippines, though, you'll discover that you can "sisig" pretty much anything. There's chicken sisig, tuna sisig, goat sisig, and even vegetarian sisig. The Squid Sisig you see here has all the hallmarks of its piggy progenitor, such as chili spice, citrus sourness and plenty of aromatic shallots and onions. Whereas the pork version features a sunny-side-up egg and crushed pork cracklings, however, this squid iteration incorporates salmon caviar and crushed prawn crackers.

MAKES 3 TO 4 SERVINGS
PREP TIME: 15 MINUTES
COOK TIME: 10 MINUTES

1 lb (500 g) cleaned fresh squid tubes and
   tentacles
3 tablespoons fresh calamansi juice
1 tablespoon dark Filipino cane vinegar
   (*sukang iloco*)
1 tablespoon oyster sauce
1 teaspoon sesame oil
1 tablespoon canola oil
1 large shallot, chopped
2 cloves garlic, chopped
1 or 2 Thai chili peppers, thinly sliced
Salt and pepper, to taste
2 green onions (scallions), thinly sliced
1 tablespoon salmon roe, plus more for serving
2 tablespoons crushed prawn crackers
Halved calamansi limes, for serving

Bring 3 quarts of water to a boil in a large pot set over high heat. Meanwhile, cut the squid tubes into ½-inch (1 cm) rings. Blanch all of the squid rings and tentacles in the boiling water for 10 seconds. Drain immediately in a large colander set in the sink and set aside.

In a large bowl, whisk together the calamansi juice, vinegar, oyster sauce, and sesame oil. Add the drained squid to the bowl and toss well to combine. Set bowl aside.

Place a large cast-iron skillet over high heat until it begins to smoke, 1 to 2 minutes. Add the canola oil and swirl to coat the bottom of the hot pan. Add the shallot, garlic and chili peppers and cook until the garlic just begins to brown, about 30 seconds. Stir in the squid and all of the liquid from the bowl and continue to cook for 1 minute more, until the squid is tender and the liquid has reduced slightly. Season to taste with salt and pepper, then scatter the green onions, salmon roe and crushed prawn crackers on top of the squid.

Remove from the heat and serve immediately in the pan while still sizzling. Offer calamansi limes alongside for squeezing, with additional salmon roe if desired. Enjoy with rice or serve with whole prawn crackers for scooping the sisig nacho-style.

UMINOM Clean, cold, and refreshing pale lagers are always a natural match with spicy and citrusy sisig. For this squid version, craft Pilsners, Helles and even Kolsch-style beers are an especially good match.

PINEAPPLE PIGS IN A BLANKET VIENNA SAUSAGE LUMPIANG SHANGHAI

This is my quick and easy version of *lumpiang Shanghai* – the diminutive Filipino spring roll most often filled with ground pork and dipped in a sweet-and-sour sauce. Just four ingredients are needed for the filling: pineapple jam, sriracha hot sauce, sliced green onions and a Vienna sausage. And because the pineapple jam and sriracha melt and mix into one another when the *lumpia* are fried, no dipping sauce is needed – it's already built into the spring roll.

MAKES 4 TO 5 SERVINGS (21 SPRING ROLLS)
PREP TIME: 25 MINUTES
COOK TIME: 10 MINUTES

21 square spring roll wrappers
   (8 x 8 in/20 x 20 cm), thawed if frozen
4 tablespoons pineapple preserves or jam
Sriracha sauce, to taste
2 green onions (scallions), thinly sliced
21 Vienna sausages (3 cans) or cocktail
   wieners
Canola oil, for frying

COOK'S NOTE The American occupation of the Philippines from 1898 to 1946 brought with it many things. One of these was the introduction of processed "convenience" foods such as Spam, Tang, instant coffee and, yes, canned Vienna sausages. Long after the Americans left, these foods are still staples in many Filipino pantries.

Rolling these small spring rolls is nearly the same as rolling the larger Pigs' Ear and Tofu Spring Rolls on page 73. However, because you're working with less filling, you'll need to tuck in some extra wrapper when rolling. Have a small dish of water on hand to seal the wrappers, and prepare a plate and a damp towel for your completed lumpia.

HOW TO ROLL

1. Place a lumpia wrapper on a clean, dry work surface so that one corner of the wrapper is pointing at you (i.e., positioned like a diamond rather than a square). Place a generous teaspoon of the pineapple jam just under the midpoint of the diamond, closest to the corner pointing at you. Squirt some sriracha sauce onto the jam, then sprinkle a few sliced green onions on top. Place one sausage horizontally over all.
2. Roll the corner closest to you up and over the filling until half of the wrapper remains.
3. Fold the left and right corners of the wrapper over the filling, folding back any excess that extends beyond the filling.
4. Using your fingers or a pastry brush, dab the edges of the wrapper with water.
5. Continue to roll the lumpia toward the final corner at the top.

Place the finished lumpia on a plate underneath a damp towel. Continue rolling until all of the filling has been used. To freeze the lumpia, place them in a single layer on a baking sheet and place in the freezer until completely frozen. Transfer the frozen lumpia to a large resealable food storage bag and store in the freezer for up to three months.

To fry the lumpia, pour oil into a large frying pan to a depth of at least 1 inch (2.5 cm). Heat the oil over high heat until it reaches 375°F (190°C) on a deep-fry thermometer. Working in batches, fry the lumpia, turning occasionally, until golden brown and crisp, 3 to 5 minutes total. (If frying frozen lumpia, fry for an additional 1 to 2 minutes.) Transfer the fried lumpia to a paper-towel-lined plate and serve immediately.

UMINOM An American IPA with tropical fruit and citrus notes will latch onto the jam in these eggrolls while also contrasting the saltiness of the sausage. Intense hop bitterness and carbonation will also help to clear the palate of any frying oil.

HOT WINGS WITH FISH SAUCE AND CALAMANSI CARAMEL

When you combine Fish Sauce and Calamansi Caramel with a few spoonfuls of Green Mango Hot Sauce, you end up with a fiery, sticky-sweet glaze that showcases the umami richness and saltiness from the fish sauce, the sourness of the calamansi and green mangoes, and the sweetness of the caramel. Pair with a bitter IPA and you've covered all five tastes!

MAKES 4 TO 6 SERVINGS
PREP TIME: 20 MINUTES
COOK TIME: 20 MINUTES FOR THE CARAMEL, PLUS 30 MINUTES TO FRY

¼ cup (65 ml) Fish Sauce and Calamansi Caramel (page 27)
1 to 2 teaspoons Green Mango Hot Sauce (page 28), or store-bought *sambal oelek* chili sauce
Canola oil, for frying
2½ lbs (1.25 kg) chicken wings
1 tablespoon chopped chives
1 tablespoon sesame seeds
Salt and freshly ground black pepper, to taste

Combine the Fish Sauce and Calamansi Caramel with the hot sauce or chili paste in a large bowl. Whisk well to mix and set aside.

Pour oil into a large frying pan or deep skillet to reach a depth of 1 inch (2.5 cm). Heat the oil over high heat until it reaches 375°F (190°C) on a deep-fry thermometer. Fry the chicken wings in batches until golden brown and crispy, about 10 minutes total per batch. Be sure to adjust the heat as necessary to maintain the temperature of the oil.

Drain the fried wings on paper towels, then transfer them to the bowl with the sauce mixture. Add the chopped chives and sesame seeds and toss until the wings are well coated with the sauce. Season with salt and pepper as needed and serve immediately.

UMINOM American pale ales and India pale ales are the way to go with these wings. Both types of ale feature citrusy hops to match the calamansi in the glaze, along with bitterness to contrast the salty-sweet caramel. Beware, though: with higher hop bitterness and higher alcohol content, IPAs can intensify spicy heat.

If you need something to cool off the fire of these hot wings, try pairing them with a Sweet Mango-Coconut Shake (page 44). The mangoes in the shake will echo the Green Mango Hot Sauce, while the coconut milk will provide soothing tongue-coating creaminess to combat the spice of the wings.

DRIED SHRIMP HUSH PUPPIES UKOY

This mashup of American hush puppies with Filipino shrimp fritters (*ukoy*) contains the best of both worlds. Tiny dried shrimp add crunch and umami to a fluffy cornmeal batter studded with spices, chilis and onions. The dried shrimp (*hibe*) can be found in Asian markets – look for the tiny variety no bigger than your thumbnail.

MAKES 3 TO 4 SERVINGS (15 TO 20 HUSH PUPPIES)
PREP TIME: 10 MINUTES
COOK TIME: 20 MINUTES

1 cup (120 g) cornmeal
1 cup (30 g) small dried shrimp
½ cup (60 g) all-purpose flour
2 teaspoons sugar
1 teaspoon baking powder
¼ teaspoon coarse sea salt
¼ teaspoon freshly ground black pepper
¼ teaspoon garlic powder
¼ teaspoon smoked paprika
1 egg
¾ cup (185 ml) coconut milk
1 red Fresno or jalapeño chili pepper,
    deseeded and diced
2 tablespoons chopped green onions
    (scallions)
Canola oil, for frying

In a large bowl, whisk together the cornmeal, shrimp, flour, sugar, baking powder, salt, black pepper, garlic powder and paprika. In a separate bowl, whisk together the egg and coconut milk, then stir in the chili pepper and green onions. Pour the wet ingredients into the large bowl with the dry ingredients and stir until just combined, being careful to not overmix. The batter should resemble a very thick cake batter.

Pour oil into a large pot or Dutch oven to reach a depth of 4 inches (10 cm). Heat the oil over high heat until it reaches 375°F (190°C) on a deep-fry thermometer, or until a bit of batter dropped into the oil begins to brown and sizzle immediately.

When the oil is ready, drop the batter into the pot by the tablespoon, working in batches as necessary. Fry, turning occasionally, until cooked through and golden brown, 4 to 5 minutes. Adjust the heat as necessary to maintain the temperature of the oil. Transfer the hush puppies to a paper-towel-lined plate. Serve immediately with Green Mango Hot Sauce (page 28) or All-Purpose Vinegar Dip (page 31).

UMINOM The moderate corn flavors in a cream ale will match the cornmeal in these hush puppies. And the slight sweetness of the cream ale will contrast the saltiness of the shrimp.

The fruit-forward sweetness and berry flavors in a California Zinfandel, along with hints of spice, will go well with the sweet and spicy notes of the hush puppies.

CHAPTER FIVE

STEAMED, STEWED, POACHED & ROASTED

In addition to steamed shellfish, gently poached sardines and oven-crisped pork belly, this chapter is where you'll find a Filipino soup of beef and tripe, and a Filipino-American chili laced with liver. Hearty stews for hardy souls in need of a stiff drink.

QUICK CALDERETA CHILI

This recipe resulted from a rare "happy accident" in the kitchen. Traditionally, *caldereta* is a Filipino beef stew with a thick sauce enriched with liver pâté. I stumbled onto this particular variation when attempting to make a caldereta with ground beef, rather than the customary chunks of beef, in an effort to save time. While I was successful in making a quick caldereta, I realized that my finished product looked exactly like American chili. So for my next attempt, I added the spices usually found in American chili, such as chili powder, cumin and cayenne. The result is this delicious Filipino-American chili laced with liver and shrimp paste and redolent of smoky spice.

MAKES 4 TO 6 SERVINGS
PREP TIME: 15 MINUTES
COOK TIME: 45 MINUTES

1 tablespoon canola oil
1 onion, diced
1 red bell pepper, diced
3 cloves garlic, chopped
1 teaspoon fermented shrimp paste (*bagoong*)
¼ teaspoon dried red pepper flakes
1½ lbs (750 g) ground beef
½ teaspoon coarse sea salt, plus more to taste
½ teaspoon freshly ground black pepper, plus more
   to taste
1 tablespoon chili powder
1 teaspoon smoked paprika
½ teaspoon ground cumin
¼ teaspoon ground red pepper (cayenne), plus
   more to taste
1 cup (250 ml) beer, preferably a pale lager
One 14.5-oz (425-ml) can diced fire-roasted tomatoes
One 8-oz (250-ml) can tomato sauce
One 4.25-oz (120-g) can prepared liverwurst spread

FOR THE GARNISH:
Grated Edam or cheddar cheese
Sliced green onions (scallions)
Chopped cilantro

Heat the oil in a large pot or Dutch oven over moderately high heat until it begins to shimmer. Stir in the onion, bell pepper, garlic, shrimp paste and dried red pepper flakes. Cook until the onion softens and turns translucent, 3 to 5 minutes. Add the beef to the pot and cook, stirring and breaking up the meat with a wooden spoon, until the meat is no longer pink, 2 to 3 minutes.

Stir in the salt, black pepper, chili powder, paprika, cumin and ground red pepper. Continue to cook until the spices become fragrant, about 1 minute. Pour in the beer and fire-roasted tomatoes and stir to combine, being sure to scrape up the browned bits from the bottom of the pot.

Combine the tomato sauce and liverwurst spread in a blender or food processor. Purée, then pour the mixture into the pot and stir. Bring the pot to a boil, then reduce the heat to low and simmer, uncovered, for 30 minutes. Taste the chili and season with more salt and pepper as needed. If you'd like a spicier chili, add more cayenne pepper. If the chili is thicker than you'd like, you can thin it out with additional beer.

Serve the chili in bowls, and garnish with cheese, green onion and cilantro as desired.

UMINOM Clean, easy-drinking pale lagers are a natural fit with chili, but for something more complex, try a Belgian-style Dubbel. The toasted malt flavors in a Dubbel play well with the chili's browned beef, while the slightly sweet, dark fruit flavors complement the richness of the liver in this chili.

On the wine side, with its sweet oak spice and cherry flavors, a Rioja is also a fine match for this chili.

VINEGAR-POACHED SARDINES PAKSIW NA ISDA

Paksiw is the Filipino cooking method of gently poaching food in vinegar. It's most often done with seafood, and was a means of preservation before the time of refrigeration. This paksiw of meaty sardines delivers a nice contrast of flavors between the oily-fleshed fish and the sharp vinegar – all highlighted by ginger, garlic and chili peppers.

MAKES 4 TO 6 SERVINGS
PREP TIME: 10 MINUTES
COOK TIME: 20 MINUTES

1 cup (250 ml) white Filipino cane vinegar (*sukang maasim*) or rice vinegar
¾ cup (185 ml) water
1-in (2.5-cm) piece of fresh ginger, peeled and cut into thin matchsticks
2 cloves garlic, smashed and peeled
½ teaspoon coarse sea salt, plus more to taste
½ teaspoon whole black peppercorns
1 or 2 Thai chili peppers, partially split in half lengthwise with stems left intact
1 bay leaf
1 lb (500 g) fresh sardines, cleaned and gutted
2 teaspoons sesame oil
Freshly ground black pepper, to taste

Combine the vinegar, water, ginger, garlic, salt, peppercorns, chili peppers and bay leaf in a large non-reactive sauté pan over high heat. Bring the liquid to a boil, reduce heat to medium-low, then cover and simmer for 10 minutes.

Uncover the pan and gently add the sardines in a single layer. Adjust the heat as necessary to maintain a steady, low simmer. Gently poach the sardines, frequently spooning the liquid over them, until just cooked through and the flesh is flaky, 5 to 6 minutes. Transfer to a serving platter along with some of the poaching liquid. Drizzle with the sesame oil and season with additional salt and freshly ground black pepper as needed.

Serve warm or at room temperature with a side of rice.

UMINOM With flavors of lemony-orange citrus and a slight sourness, a Saison can harmonize with these sardines without being overpowered by the tartness from the vinegar. The black-pepper notes in a Saison bridge nicely to the black pepper in the sardines as well, while the beer's high effervescence and dry finish are great for cutting through the oily richness of the fish.

BEER-STEAMED BLUE CRABS

A bunch of cilantro, some lemongrass, and a few bottles of cheap beer (save the good stuff for drinking) are all you need for a crab-crackin', newspaper-tabletop-coverin' good time. (Well, I guess you would need crabs and newspaper for all that, too.)

MAKES 4 TO 6 SERVINGS
PREP TIME: 5 MINUTES
COOK TIME: 20 MINUTES

1 bunch cilantro
3 stalks lemongrass
2-in (5-cm) piece of fresh ginger, sliced into thin coins
Three 12-oz (355-ml) bottles beer, preferably a light lager
12 live blue crabs

Spread the cilantro across the bottom of a pot or Dutch oven large enough to hold all of the crabs. Cut the lemongrass stalks in half, then pound the bottom white portion of each stalk with a mallet or the back of a knife. Place the lemongrass stalks in the bottom of the pot in a crisscross pattern to form a bed for the crabs. Add the sliced ginger to the pot and pour in all of the beer.

Place the pot over high heat and bring the liquid to a boil. Once it boils, add the live crabs to the pot and cover with lid. Steam until the shells of the crabs turn bright red-orange, about 10 to 15 minutes.

Transfer the crabs to a large platter. Serve immediately with Spicy Fish Sauce and Calamansi Dipping Sauce (page 26) and a side of rice on a table covered with newspaper for easy cleanup.

UMINOM Be sure you have plenty of Pilsner beer on hand to serve with these crabs on your newspaper-covered tabletop. Its clean, balanced flavors won't overpower the natural sweetness of the crabmeat, and it has just enough floral aromatics to complement the lemongrass, cilantro and ginger, along with snappy bitterness and carbonation to cleanse the palate.

For the wine lovers at your crab-crackin' party, bottles of Pinot Gris will provide bright citrus and tropical fruit notes to complement the aromatics in the steaming pot, while contrasting the sweet crab meat and salty-sour dipping sauce.

COOK'S NOTE Female crabs are prized because they are sometimes filled with delectable crab roe. To identify the sex of a crab, turn it over and look for one of two Washington, D.C. landmarks on its belly. If it has the domed capital building (as shown on page 82) it's a female crab. If it has the long and pointy Washington Monument, it's a male crab – still just as tasty, except without any roe.

BEER-AND-SPAM MAC AND CHEESE

J. Kenji López-Alt, chief culinary advisor at the *Serious Eats* website and author of the cookbook *The Food Lab: Better Home Cooking through Science*, originally posted a "3-Ingredient, 10-Minute Macaroni and Cheese" recipe on *Serious Eats* that caught my eye. What are those three ingredients (not counting salt and water)? Macaroni, cheese and canned evaporated milk. Considering that canned evaporated milk is a staple ingredient in many a Filipino pantry, I was immediately drawn to Kenji's recipe.

Sure enough, when I looked in my cupboard to make Kenji's Mac and Cheese, there were indeed a couple of cans of evaporated milk, as well as a few cans of Spam, as it happened. One thing led to another, and I ended up with a Filipinized version of Kenji's recipe that featured the aforementioned evaporated milk and Spam, as well as a splash of beer and some shredded *queso de bola* Edam cheese.

Although my version of Kenji's recipe has more than three ingredients, it still comes together in no time, and it goes incredibly well with beer. And depending on how hungry you and your drinking companions are, this recipe can be easily scaled up or down.

MAKES 2 TO 4 SERVINGS
PREP TIME: 10 MINUTES
COOK TIME: 25 MINUTES

1 tablespoon oil

6 oz (170 g) cubed Spam

¼ cup (65 ml) beer, preferably a pale lager

6 oz (170 g) elbow macaroni

1 cup (250 ml) water, or as needed

Pinch of salt, plus more to taste

¾ cup (180 ml) evaporated milk

6 oz (170 g) grated cheese, preferably an equal mix of Edam and mild cheddar, or all mild cheddar

Hot sauce (optional), for serving

Heat the oil in a large skillet or saucepan over medium-high heat. When the oil begins to shimmer, add the Spam to the pan in a single layer and cook, undisturbed, for 1 to 2 minutes until the first side is browned and crisp. If you try to stir the Spam before it browns properly, it may stick to the pan.

After the first side has browned, stir and toss the Spam so that the other surfaces are coated in the oil. Continue to toss and cook for 1 to 2 minute more to lightly brown and crisp on all sides. Transfer to a plate lined with paper towels and set aside.

Return the pan to medium-high heat and pour in the beer. Use a wooden spoon to stir and scrape up any browned bits that may be stuck to the bottom.

Add the macaroni, and then pour in just enough cold water to barely cover. Increase the heat to high, add a pinch of salt, and bring the liquid to a boil. Continue to cook, stirring frequently, until the liquid has been almost completely absorbed and the macaroni is nearly al dente, 5 to 6 minutes.

Add the evaporated milk and bring to a boil. Reduce the heat to low, add the cheese, and stir continuously until all the cheese has melted and a creamy sauce has formed, about 2 minutes more. The sauce will thicken as it sits; add a splash of beer or water to thin as needed.

Return the Spam to the pan and stir to incorporate. Season to taste with more salt, and serve immediately with hot sauce on the side if desired.

 **UMINOM** Keep this Spam dish classy by pairing it with a Brass Donkey cocktail (page 42). The sweetness of the mango juice is a nice foil to the salty Spam, while the bubbly malt liquor helps to cut the richness of the cheese.

For a beer pairing, malty brown ales are always a great match for cheddar and nutty cheeses like Edam.

BEEF, TRIPE AND GINGER SOUP IPA PAPAITAN

Hailing from the Ilocos region of the Northern Philippines, the bracingly bitter soup known as *Papaitan* is a source of local pride, and what many consider to be the ultimate pulutan. In fact, it was a favorite of my late grandfather, Juan, who usually drank a can of Keystone alongside his Papaitan.

The most hardcore versions of Papaitan are usually comprised of the organ meats found within a goat, or cow, such as stomach and intestines, as well as bitter bile (see cook's note). But the more common household versions usually only feature beef and tripe, which is what I use in this recipe.

Although beef bile can be easily found at Asian markets, I realize that's a hard ask for even the most adventurous cook. But not to worry, you can make a deliciously bitter Papaitan at home by simply reducing a bottle of bitter IPA beer in the soup! And while bitterness is definitely the hallmark of a good Papaitan, it's also an incredibly complex dish. Spicy and fragrant with ginger and chilies, packed with umami and saltiness from fish sauce, and bright and tart after a finishing squeeze of citrus, Papaitan can bring about a new world of flavors and textures to those brave enough to try it. *Mabuhay! Tagay! Agbiag!*

MAKES 4 TO 6 SERVINGS
PREP TIME: 25 MINUTES
COOK TIME: 3 HOURS, 30 MINUTES

1 lb (500 g) beef honeycomb tripe
2 tablespoons canola oil
2 lbs (1 kg) whole boneless beef chuck roast, cut into 2 steaks
Coarse sea salt, to taste
Freshly ground black pepper, to taste
1 onion, diced
3-in (7.5-cm) piece fresh ginger, peeled and cut into thin matchsticks
3 cloves garlic, minced
¼ teaspoon dried red pepper flakes
One 12-oz. (375-ml) bottle of beer, preferably an India pale ale
1 tablespoon fish sauce
2 bay leaves
1 or 2 Thai chili peppers, split in half lengthwise with stems still intact

1–2 tablespoons beef bile (optional)
Freshly squeezed calamansi juice, or lemon juice, to taste

FOR SERVING:
Sliced Thai chili peppers
Calamansi lime halves, or lemon wedges
Sliced green onions (scallions)

UMINOM A big, bold and bitter IPA is just the beer that can match the intensity of this soup. Be aware though, that the hop bitterness in the beer can magnify the heat and spice from the chili peppers.

To contrast the bitterness in the soup, and for something a bit more cooling, you'll do just as well with an icy Filipino lager in your hand.

Slice the tripe into small, thin strips about 1 inch (2.5 cm) long by ½ inch (1.25 cm) wide. Place the tripe in a medium pot and cover with cold water. Bring the pot to a boil over high heat, reduce heat to low, then simmer for 10 minutes. Drain the tripe in a large colander set in the sink and rinse with cold running water. Set the tripe aside. Wash and dry the pot. Heat the oil in the cleaned pot over moderately high heat. Season the beef on all sides with salt and pepper, then, working in batches, add the beef to the pot. Cook until the meat is brown and crusty, 4–5 minutes per side. Transfer the browned beef to a platter and set aside.

Add the onion to the pot and cook until soft and translucent, about 5 minutes. Add the ginger, garlic, and dried red pepper flakes, and cook for 2–3 minutes more until fragrant. Pour in the bottle of beer, stirring to scrape up any browned bits from the bottom of the pot. Bring the beer to a boil and continue cooking until the beer is reduced by half, about 3 minutes.

Meanwhile, cut the beef into bite-sized ½-inch (1.25-cm) cubes. Return the beef and the tripe to the pot, then add enough cold water to cover everything by an inch (2.5 cm). Stir in the fish sauce, bay leaves, and the split chili peppers. Bring everything to a boil, then reduce the heat to low and simmer, partially covered, for 2–3 hours until the beef and tripe are tender.

Stir in the beef bile, if using, and simmer for another 5 minutes. Taste the soup, and season with salt, black pepper, and calamansi or lemon juice as desired. Serve immediately with sliced Thai chili peppers, calamansi lime halves or lemon wedges, and sliced green onions (scallions) on the side.

COOK'S NOTE Beef bile, as pictured to the left, can be found frozen at many Asian markets and Filipino markets.

Biologically speaking, bile is a greenish fluid that is secreted by the liver and stored in the gallbladder to aid in the digestion of grass (that's why beef bile is green). Culinarily speaking, it's bitter as hell. A spoonful of beef bile is a nuclear bomb of bitterness, so a little goes a long way.

Using animal bile as a bittering agent in food is not exclusive to the Philippines, as it is also used in Thailand and other Southeast Asian countries.

CRISPY OVEN–ROASTED PORK BELLY LECHON KAWALI

The only thing better than crispy deep-fried pork belly is discovering that you can get crispy pork belly without deep-frying it. Salting the pork belly, scoring the skin, and air-drying overnight in the refrigerator all help to achieve crunchy skin. Lastly, starting the pork belly at a lower temperature in the oven allows the meat to gently roast without becoming dried out. A final blast of intense high heat in the oven makes the skin bubble and puff for its final crispy *chicharrón* texture.

MAKES 4 TO 6 SERVINGS
PREP TIME: 20 MINUTES
COOK TIME: 1 HOUR, 15 MINUTES

2 tablespoons coarse sea salt, divided
1 teaspoon coarsely ground black pepper
3 stalks lemongrass, very roughly chopped
One 2.5-lb (1.25-kg) slab of skin-on pork belly

UMINOM An ice-cold San Miguel Filipino lager is as nostalgic a match as you will find for crispy, fatty Lechon Kawali. But for a more interesting and flavorful accompaniment, look for craft-brewed Pilsners. These usually feature more malt and hop character than standard industrial lagers.

The pre-roast rest on a bed of black pepper and lemongrass makes this Lechon Kawali particularly wonderful with Saison – an ale with trademark notes of black pepper and floral lemony flavors.

The crisp acidity and slight sweetness of white Zinfandel and rosé wines are great counterpoints to the crunchy, salty skin and rich fat of roast pork.

Place 1 tablespoon of the salt, along with the black pepper and lemongrass, in the bottom of a shallow baking dish large enough to hold the pork belly. Stir with fingers to mix.

Using a sharp paring knife, score the pork belly skin every ½ inch (1.25 cm) horizontally, and every ½ inch (1.25 cm) vertically to form a crosshatch pattern. Be sure to just cut through the skin to the fat, not all the way through to the meat.

Place the pork belly, skin-side-up, into the baking dish so that the meat is in direct contact with the spices and lemongrass. Rub the remaining 1 tablespoon of salt into the skin of the pork belly, making sure to rub salt into the cuts in the skin. Refrigerate overnight, uncovered, in the baking dish.

The next day, preheat the oven to 350°F (175°C).

Remove the pork belly from the baking dish and brush off as much of the spices and lemongrass as possible from the bottom – it's okay if some remains. Blot the skin of the pork belly with a paper towel. It's okay if some salt remains on the skin as well.

Place the pork belly skin-side up on a wire rack set inside a foil-lined sheet pan. Place on the middle rack of the preheated oven and roast for 45 minutes.

Remove the pork belly from the oven, brush the skin with some of the fat that dripped onto the sheet pan and set aside. Increase the oven temperature to 550°F (290°C), or to the highest temperature it can go. Once the oven has come up to temperature, return the pork belly to the oven and continue to roast, checking every 5 minutes, until the skin becomes puffy and crisp all over, 15 to 20 minutes. If you notice that some parts of the skin are not getting crisp, rotate the pan as necessary.

Remove the pork belly from the oven and allow to rest for 5 minutes. Place the pork belly on a cutting board and cut into bite-sized chunks. Serve immediately with All-Purpose Vinegar Dip (page 31), Green Mango Hot Sauce (page 28), or Garlic Bagoong Aioli (page 29).

BEER-STEAMED CLAMS WITH SPAM

Consider this my highbrow-lowbrow, spicy-salty, rhyme-time, surf-and-Astroturf dish, perfect for a beer and a cocktail. I don't think anything else needs to be said. Enjoy.

MAKES 4 TO 6 SERVINGS
PREP TIME: 10 MINUTES
COOK TIME: 20 MINUTES

2 tablespoons canola oil
12 oz (340 g) Spam, diced
1 tablespoon chopped shallots
1 tablespoon chopped garlic
¼ teaspoon dried red pepper flakes
1 tablespoon tomato paste
½ cup (125 ml) beer, preferably a pale lager
2 tablespoons fresh calamansi juice or lime juice
2½ lbs (1.25 kg) fresh clams, cleaned and scrubbed
Freshly ground black pepper, to taste
Coarse sea salt, to taste
1 tablespoon chopped chives, for garnish
Crusty bread, for serving

Heat the oil in a large pot over moderately high heat. Add the Spam and stir to coat with oil. Cook, stirring frequently, until lightly browned, 3 to 4 minutes. Add the shallots, garlic and red pepper flakes and continue to cook, stirring frequently, until the shallots soften and the garlic just begins to brown, about 2 minutes. Add the tomato paste and cook, stirring frequently, until the tomato paste begins to brown, about 2 minutes.

Pour in the beer and calamansi juice and stir, scraping up any browned bits from the bottom of the pot. Immediately add all of the clams to the pot. Increase the heat to high, cover the pot and steam until the clams just begin to open, 3 to 5 minutes.

Remove the pot from the heat, uncover and stir until all ingredients are well combined and the clams are coated in the sauce. Season to taste with black pepper. Keep in mind that the liquid released by the clams is salty, so additional salt may not be needed.

Transfer the entire contents of the pot to a large serving platter and garnish with the chopped chives. Serve with cocktail forks or toothpicks, along with crusty bread or toasted Filipino *pan de sal* rolls for dipping in the sauce.

UMINOM For something with just enough snappy bite to contrast the saltiness of the Spam without overpowering the clams, go for a hoppy Pilsner beer. A Hefeweizen will boost the umami character in the tomato paste and contrast the saltiness of the clams and Spam. For something a bit stronger, pair this dish with a Belgian strong golden ale. The dry yet fruity effervescence of this ale is a great counterpoint to the briny clams and salty Spam. A low level of spicy hop character, along with a high alcohol level, will intensify the heat of the dried red pepper flakes in this dish, so beware.

On the cocktail side of things, the Miguel in Hell (page 45) has some spiciness of its own to match the dried red pepper flakes here, as well as salty-sour notes to match the clam sauce.

ADOBO–STEAMED MUSSELS ADOBONG TAHONG

No long braising time is needed for this quick-cooking *adobo*. A splash of soy and vinegar are all these mussels need to steam open. A finishing splash of coconut milk enriches the sauce while taming the heat of the chilies and easing the sharpness of the vinegar.

MAKES 2 TO 4 SERVINGS
PREP TIME: 10 MINUTES
COOK TIME: 25 MINUTES

2 tablespoons canola oil

1 tablespoon minced lemongrass

1 tablespoon minced garlic

¼ teaspoon freshly ground black pepper, plus more to taste

1 or 2 Thai chili peppers, thinly sliced

1 bay leaf

1 tablespoon soy sauce

¼ cup (65 ml) white Filipino cane vinegar (*sukang maasim*)

¼ cup (65 ml) water

2½ lbs (1.25 kg) fresh mussels in the shell, scrubbed, rinsed and beards removed

¼ cup (65 ml) coconut milk

Coarse sea salt, to taste

1 tablespoon chopped parsley, for garnish

Crusty bread, for serving

Heat the oil in a large pot over moderately high heat. Add the lemongrass, garlic, black pepper, chili peppers and bay leaf. Cook, stirring frequently, until the garlic just begins to brown, about 2 minutes. Pour in the soy sauce, vinegar and water, stirring to scrape up any browned bits from the bottom of the pot. Immediately add all of the mussels to the pot. Increase the heat to high, cover the pot and steam the mussels until they just begin to open, 5 to 7 minutes.

Using tongs or a slotted spoon, transfer the opened mussels to a bowl or large rimmed platter, making sure to leave as much liquid in the pot as possible, along with the bay leaf. Set the mussels aside.

Whisk the coconut milk into the pot and bring to a boil. Continue boiling, uncovered, until the liquid is reduced by half – depending on how much liquid the mussels have released, this will take anywhere from 5 to 10 minutes. When the sauce is reduced, taste for seasoning and add salt and additional pepper as needed. Keep in mind that the liquid released by the mussels is salty, so you may not need additional salt.

Remove and discard the bay leaf and pour the sauce over the mussels. Garnish with the chopped parsley and serve with crusty bread or toasted Filipino *pan de sal* rolls for dipping in the sauce.

UMINOM Witbier is a classic pairing with mussels, and it's especially good with this coconut-enriched adobo version. Bright with citrus flavors and low lactic acidity, a Witbier not only syncs up with the vinegar in the adobo sauce, but it also helps to cut through the rich coconut milk.

CHAPTER SIX

OFF THE GRILL

Charred by flame and kissed by smoke, the recipes in this section deliver a range of Filipino flavors that can only be brought about by an open flame. So grab a cold drink, fire up your barbecue, and get grilling! Your guests are waiting!

BEEF SKEWERS WITH CITRUS AND ONIONS BISTEK

With calamansi lime, soy sauce and onions, all the flavors of a classic Filipino *bistek* are here, but in easy-to-eat, pulutan-friendly skewer form.

MAKES 4 TO 6 SERVINGS
PREP TIME: 30 MINUTES
COOK TIME: 15 MINUTES

1½ lbs (750 g) beef sirloin, cut into 1-inch
　(2.5-cm) cubes
¼ cup (65 ml) fresh calamansi juice
¼ cup (65 ml) soy sauce
1 tablespoon molasses
1 tablespoon Worcestershire sauce
¼ teaspoon freshly ground black pepper
2 green onions (scallions), cut into 1-in
　(2.5-cm) lengths

Ten 4-in (10-cm) bamboo skewers

Place the beef in a large resealable plastic bag and set aside.

In a small bowl, whisk together the calamansi juice, soy sauce, molasses, Worcestershire sauce and black pepper. Pour the marinade into the bag with the beef and seal, pressing out as much air as possible. Marinate in the refrigerator for at least 4 hours or overnight.

Soak the skewers in water for at least 30 minutes prior to grilling. Preheat grill for direct cooking.

Remove the beef from the marinade. Thread the beef and green onions onto the skewers, alternating between beef and green onion segments. Place skewers on the grill over direct high heat and grill, turning and rotating frequently, until the beef is well seared all over, 2 to 3 minutes per side for medium-rare. Remove the skewers from the grill and serve immediately.

UMINOM American brown ales feature bright citrus hop aromatics to echo the calamansi juice in the marinade; the malty-sweet toasty flavors in these beers bridge nicely to the molasses and char on the beef.

A high-acid red wine, like a juicy Barbera, will marry with the calamansi juice while also helping to cut the richness of the beef.

GRILLED CHICKEN LIVERS INIHAW NA ATAY

When it comes to grilling chicken livers, it's a thin line between tender and chalky, so watch these skewers like a hawk. When finished, the livers should be charred and dark on the outside, yet still moist and slightly pink on the inside.

MAKES 4 TO 6 SERVINGS
PREP TIME: 30 MINUTES
COOK TIME: 5 MINUTES

1 lb (500 g) chicken livers
¼ cup (65 ml) soy sauce
¼ cup (65 ml) fresh calamansi juice,
   or lime juice, plus more to taste
1 tablespoon chopped garlic
2 tablespoons chopped cilantro, divided
1 teaspoon brown sugar
1 teaspoon sesame oil
¼ teaspoon freshly ground black pepper
Coarse sea salt, to taste

Six 12-inch (30-cm) bamboo or metal skewers

UMINOM Sweet, sour and incredibly complex, Flanders brown ales *(oud bruins)* feature a number of flavor matches with these grilled liver skewers. The prune and raisin sweetness in the beer nicely complements the richness of the liver, contrasts the salty soy sauce and echoes the brown sugar in the marinade. The sourness and tannic acidity of the beer also help to highlight the brightness of the calamansi.
   For wine, a Pinot Gris delivers a touch of residual sweetness and bright acidity to complement the richness of the chicken livers.

Place the chicken livers in a shallow baking dish. In a medium bowl, combine the soy sauce, calamansi juice, garlic, 1 tablespoon of the cilantro, brown sugar, sesame oil and black pepper and whisk well to blend. Pour the marinade over the chicken livers, place in the refrigerator, and marinate for 2 hours.

   If using bamboo skewers, soak them in water for at least 30 minutes prior to grilling. Preheat a grill for direct cooking.

   Remove the chicken livers from the marinade, discarding the marinade. Divide the chicken livers equally among the skewers. Grill over direct heat, turning frequently, until browned and cooked through yet still tender (they should still be slightly pink on the inside), 4 to 5 minutes total.

   Remove the skewers from the grill. Squeeze more calamansi juice over them, sprinkle with salt to taste, and garnish with the rest of the cilantro. Serve immediately.

GRILLED COCONUT AND LEMONGRASS SHRIMP

Bathed in a fragrant coconut-milk marinade and grilled with their shells on, these shrimp remain moist and flavorful even after a quick char over open flames. And yes, you can and should eat the shells.

MAKES 4 TO 6 SERVINGS
PREP TIME: 30 MINUTES
COOK TIME: 5 MINUTES

1 lb (500 g) large, shell-on shrimp

1 stalk lemongrass, minced

2 tablespoons fresh calamansi juice
    or lime juice

1 tablespoon fish sauce

1 to 2 teaspoons *sambal oelek* chili paste

1 tsp brown sugar

¼ cup (65 ml) coconut milk

Salt and freshly ground black pepper, to taste

Calamansi limes or lime wedges, for serving

Bamboo skewers (optional)

UMINOM Gose, a sour wheat beer from Germany, delivers a tart acidity that will hook onto the calamansi juice while contrasting and cutting through the coconut milk in these shrimp. But perhaps the most intriguing thing about Gose is its slight but noticeable saltiness – a perfect note to highlight both the fish sauce in the marinade and the natural brininess of the shrimp.

The crisp, light mouthfeel of an unoaked Chardonnay contrasts and cuts through the creamy coconut milk marinade, while still providing bright acidity and citrus notes to complement the calamansi and lemongrass.

Place the shrimp in a large resealable plastic food storage bag and set aside. Combine the lemongrass, juice, fish sauce, chili paste, sugar and coconut milk in a medium bowl and whisk to blend.

Reserve ¼ cup (65 ml) of the marinade in a lidded container and refrigerate. Pour the remaining marinade into the bag with the shrimp and seal, pressing out as much air as possible. Marinate in the refrigerator for 1 to 2 hours.

If using bamboo skewers, soak in water for at least 30 minutes prior to grilling. The shrimp may also be grilled without skewers. Preheat the grill for direct cooking.

Place the shrimp on the grill over direct high heat. Grill, turning and frequently brushing with the reserved marinade, until the shrimp turn bright pink and are charred, 2 to 3 minutes per side. Remove the shrimp from the grill, season with salt and pepper to taste and serve with calamansi limes to squeeze over.

GRILLED LONG BEANS INIHAW NA SITAO

This is my favorite way to cook long beans. A quick marinade in Filipino vinegar and fermented shrimp paste provides acid and umami, while a quick char on the grill brings out the natural sweetness in the beans. And because these beans are super long, you are less likely to lose any between the grates of your grill – just keep everything perpendicular.

MAKES 4 TO 6 SERVINGS
PREP TIME: 5 MINUTES
COOK TIME: 5 MINUTES

1 lb (500 g) long beans, ends trimmed
3 cloves garlic, minced
¼ teaspoon dried red pepper flakes
2 teaspoons fermented shrimp paste (*bagoong*)
1 tablespoon Filipino dark cane vinegar (*sukang iloco*)
1 tablespoon olive oil
Zest of 1 lemon
Fresh lemon juice, to taste
Coarse sea salt and freshly ground black pepper, to taste

Preheat the grill for direct cooking.

Spread the long beans out on a foil-lined sheet pan and set aside.

In a medium bowl, combine the garlic, red pepper flakes, shrimp paste, vinegar and olive oil and whisk well to combine. Pour the marinade over the long beans, then use your hands to massage the marinade into the long beans until they are evenly coated.

Place the long beans on the grill over direct heat. Grill, turning frequently with tongs, until charred and tender, about 5 minutes. Transfer to a large platter, then scatter the lemon zest over. Squeeze fresh lemon juice on the beans to taste, and season with salt and pepper as needed. You can choose to cut the long beans into bite-sized pieces at this point, but I like to serve them whole, as they are nearly tender enough to be slurped up like thick noodles.

UMINOM Grilled veggies are always great with Vienna-style lagers, and these long beans are no exception. The firm hop bitterness of the beer is just enough to cut through the rich umami of the dressing, while the delicate malt sweetness and toastiness will harmonize nicely with the sweetness and char on the beans.

GRILLED BACON SKEWERS WITH PINEAPPLE GLAZE ISAW

Isaw is a grilled Filipino delicacy featuring the small intestines of a chicken (or a pig, depending on the preference of the griller). The intestines are squished onto skewers in a serpentine zig-zag pattern, grilled over fiery coals and enjoyed with any number of *sawsawan* sauces such as spicy vinegar or sweet-and-sour sauce.

Charred and crispy on the outside, tender and chewy on the inside and smoky all over, grilled chicken guts on a stick are a wondrously delicious thing. Trouble is, chicken intestines can be hard to come by – even finding them at my local mom-and-pop Filipino market is spotty at best. Luckily, I discovered that bacon (of course, bacon) can deliver the same crispy, chewy textures and smoky flavors as the more traditional chicken intestines. And with a sweet and sour glaze of pineapple, citrus and vinegar, these bacon "*isaw*" skewers don't need a dipping sauce, but for a spicy kick you can't go wrong with Green Mango Hot Sauce (page 28).

MAKES 4 TO 6 SERVINGS
PREP TIME: 30 MINUTES
COOK TIME: 15 MINUTES

1 lb (500 g) thick-sliced bacon
2 tablespoons pineapple preserves or jam
1 tablespoon fresh calamansi juice or lime juice
1 tablespoon coconut vinegar (*sukang tuba*) or distilled white vinegar
¼ teaspoon red pepper flakes
Freshly ground black pepper, to taste

Six 12-inch (30-cm) bamboo or metal skewers

Skewer the bacon as described in the steps on the facing page. Combine the pineapple preserves, calamansi juice, coconut vinegar and red pepper flakes in a small bowl to make the glaze.

Place the bacon skewers on the cool side of the grill and brush on some of the glaze. Continue to grill over indirect heat, turning and rotating the skewers frequently, until much of the fat renders off, about 10 minutes total.

Working in batches, move some of the skewers to the hot side of the grill over direct heat. Brush with additional glaze while turning the skewers frequently. Continue to grill until nicely browned, glazed and charred, 3 to 4 minutes total. Repeat until all skewers have been cooked over direct heat. Because there is so much fat in the bacon, the flames from the grill will flare up, so be careful to turn and rotate the skewers from the hot to cool side of the grill as necessary.

Remove the skewers from the grill and season with freshly ground black pepper. Serve immediately.

COOK'S NOTE If using bamboo skewers, soak them in water for at least 30 minutes prior to grilling. Preheat a grill for indirect cooking.

UMINOM The tropical fruit flavors in IPAs and double IPAs are a perfect match for the pineapple glaze on these skewers; the high hop bitterness and alcohol in these beers serve to cut through the fat and saltiness of the bacon.

With a mix of sweet fruit juices that complement the pineapple glaze on these skewers, as well as dark Jamaican rum with smoky molasses notes to highlight the bacon, a cold glass of Panantukan Punch (page 40) makes a knockout accompaniment.

HOW TO SKEWER BACON

Yes, there are simpler ways to place a slice of bacon onto a skewer (not that this way is at all difficult), but I find that this particular method best mimics the zig-zag appearance of a traditional Filipino isaw skewer of chicken intestines. If using bamboo skewers, soak them in water for at least 30 minutes prior to grilling.

1. Fold a slice of bacon in half lengthwise.
2. Bunch up the length of bacon in a zig-zag fashion, like an accordion.
3. Carefully push the skewer through the center of the bacon, making sure to pierce each fold.
4. Repeat steps 1–3 with a second slice of bacon. Spread apart the bacon on the skewer so that it isn't bunched together too tightly. Repeat with additional skewers until all of the bacon has been skewered.

BEER-MARINATED CHICKEN SKEWERS WITH SHRIMP PASTE RUB

Benefiting from both a beer marinade and a fermented shrimp-paste spice rub, these chicken skewers are tender and packed with flavor. They will not disappoint!

MAKES 4 TO 6 SERVINGS
PREP TIME: 30 MINUTES
COOK TIME: 10 MINUTES

FOR THE MARINADE:

2 lbs (1 kg) boneless, skinless chicken thighs, cut into 1-inch (2.5-cm) cubes
¼ cup (65 ml) fresh calamansi juice, or lemon juice
¼ cup (65 ml) coconut vinegar (*sukang tuba*) or white distilled vinegar
¼ cup (65 ml) soy sauce
½ cup (125 ml) beer, preferably a light lager
1 tablespoon minced garlic
1 tablespoon minced lemongrass

FOR THE RUB:

1 teaspoon garlic powder
1 teaspoon sweet paprika
1 teaspoon smoked paprika
2 teaspoons brown sugar
1 teaspoons shrimp paste (*bagoong*)

Ten 12-inch (30-cm) bamboo or metal skewers

Arrange the chicken in a single layer in a large baking dish. Combine the remaining marinade ingredients in a large bowl and whisk to combine. Pour the marinade over the chicken and marinate in the refrigerator for at least 4 hours or overnight.

If using bamboo skewers, soak in water for at least 30 minutes prior to grilling. Preheat a grill for direct cooking.

Drain off and discard the marinade from the chicken, then thread the chicken onto the skewers and set aside.

Combine all rub ingredients in a small bowl and mix well to form a paste. Massage the rub all over the chicken with your hands, making sure to distribute it evenly.

Place the chicken skewers on the grill over direct heat and grill, turning frequently, until cooked through and charred, 7 to 10 minutes total. Serve immediately.

UMINOM A clean, crisp lager, such as a Pilsner, is always a welcome sight at any Filipino barbecue. In this case, the balance of malt and hops won't stand in the way of the bright marinade or the savory rub, but will provide enough of a counterpoint with mild sweetness and bitterness. The bright flavors of citrus and lemongrass in these chicken skewers will sing when paired with a lemony Witbier. The same citrus in the Witbier is also a great foil to the flavorful shrimp-paste rub.

GRILLED GARLIC LAMB CHOPS SALPICAO

Because of their dainty size, lamb chops make for a great quick-cooking finger food to serve alongside a beer or glass of wine. These *salpicao* lamb chops are marinated in a pungent paste of garlic, fish sauce and soy sauce, then quickly charred on a hot grill.

MAKES 3 TO 4 SERVINGS
PREP TIME: 15 MINUTES
COOK TIME: 5 MINUTES

8 lamb rib chops, about 2 lbs (1 kg) total
8 cloves garlic, smashed and peeled
1 teaspoon soy sauce
1 teaspoon fish sauce
½ teaspoon freshly ground black pepper, plus more to taste
¼ cup (65 ml) olive oil
Coarse sea salt, to taste
1 tablespoon chopped chives, for garnish

Place the lamb chops in a single layer in a shallow dish and set aside.

Combine the garlic, soy sauce, fish sauce, black pepper and olive oil in a food processor and process to make a thick paste. Pour over the lamb chops, turning to ensure even coverage. Marinate at room temperature for 1 to 2 hours.

Preheat a grill for direct cooking.

Remove the lamb chops from the marinade and grill over direct heat until nicely charred on all sides, 2 to 3 minutes per side for medium-rare. Transfer to a serving dish, season with salt and pepper and garnish with chopped chives.

UMINOM The toasted malt flavors in a Belgian Dubbel will accentuate the char on these chops, while its slightly sweet, dark fruit flavors will complement the lamb's gaminess. The moderate bitterness of the Dubbel is enough to cut through the fat of the lamb, and also highlights the garlicky bite in the marinade. For wine, look to the savory, rich, and dark fruit flavors of a Sangiovese to match the richness of these lamb chops.

GRILLED PORK BELLY SKEWERS WITH COFFEE AND GINGER BEER GLAZE

Before candied bacon ever became a "thing," Filipinos had *liempo*-cue: rich, fatty cubes of pork belly threaded onto skewers, grilled over an open flame and brushed with a sticky-sweet glaze usually made from cola or lemon-lime soda.

In place of soda, my version of liempo-cue relies on ginger beer – not only for sweetness, but for a spicy, gingery bite as well. I also find that the addition of coffee and molasses provides a depth of flavor that plays well with the smoke from the grill.

MAKES 6 SERVINGS
PREP TIME: 30 MINUTES
COOK TIME: 20 MINUTES

2 lbs (1 kg) fresh skinless pork belly

12 oz (355 ml) ginger beer or ginger ale

1 cup (250 ml) strong brewed coffee

4 tablespoons soy sauce

2 tablespoons molasses

¼ teaspoon freshly ground black pepper

2-inch (5-cm) piece fresh ginger, peeled and
    cut into thin matchsticks

1 tablespoon brown sugar

Six 12-inch (30-cm) bamboo or metal skewers

Place the pork belly in the freezer for 20 to 30 minutes to make it easier to slice. Remove from the freezer and cut into pieces 1 inch (2.5 cm) square and ½ inch (1.25 cm) thick. Arrange in a single layer in a large baking dish.

In a large bowl, whisk together the ginger beer, coffee, soy sauce, molasses, black pepper and ginger. Reserve 1 cup of the marinade and refrigerate in a lidded container. Pour the remaining marinade over the pork, then cover and refrigerate overnight.

If using bamboo skewers, soak them in water for at least 30 minutes prior to grilling. Preheat a grill for indirect cooking.

Remove the pork from the marinade, discarding the used marinade. Thread the pork onto skewers and set aside.

Combine the 1 cup reserved marinade and the brown sugar in a small saucepan over high heat and bring to a boil. Continue to boil, stirring frequently, until the liquid is reduced by half and thickened to a glaze, 5 to 10 minutes. Remove from the heat and set aside.

Place the pork belly skewers on the cool side of the grill and brush glaze on all sides. Continue to grill the pork over indirect heat, turning and rotating the skewers frequently, until much of the fat has rendered off, about 10 minutes total.

Working in batches, move some of the skewers to the hot side of the grill over direct heat. Brush the pork with more glaze while turning the skewers frequently. Continue to grill until nicely browned, glazed, and charred, 4 to 5 minutes total. Repeat until all skewers have been grilled over direct heat. Because there is so much fat in the pork belly, the flames from the grill will flare up, so be careful to keep rotating the skewers from the hot side of the grill to the cool part as necessary.

Serve with a side of rice, along with Green Mango Hot Sauce (page 28) or Grilled Tomato and Green Onion Skewers (page 52).

UMINOM A nice cold bottle of ginger beer or ginger ale is perfect with these gingery pork skewers.

For a higher-octane accompaniment, the roasted bitter coffee notes in a porter or stout would harmonize nicely with the coffee in the glaze. A German Rauchbier, with smoky bacon aromas, would also be great with these charred pork skewers.

As for wine, a sparkling red Lambrusco goes surprisingly well with these skewers.

The light fruit and acidity in this bubbly red complements the sweetness of the glaze, while the bubbles help to cut through the richness of the pork.

CHAPTER SEVEN

SWEET TREATS

A dessert section in a cookbook about
Filipino appetizers and bar food? Of course.
Filipinos don't stop drinking when the sweets
come to the table, and neither should you!

HEAVENLY BEER AND PEANUT BRITTLE

In a city called Baguio in the northern Philippines is the Good Shepherd Convent, where visitors are more likely to pay for tasty snacks than they are to pay any sort of homage. You see, the Good Shepherd Convent gift shop sells a number of delicious fruit jams, jellies and preserves made by the nuns that live in the convent. But for me, the best item at Good Shepherd is the nuns' famous peanut brittle – a thin, easy-on-the-teeth candy that is sweet, caramelly, and laden with chopped peanuts.

Although the peanut brittle made by the kind sisters at Good Shepherd is indeed divine, making your own at home is much easier than booking a flight to the Philippines. To intensify the dark caramel flavors in peanut brittle, my version includes a dark, malty and rich Doppelbock – a centuries-old beer traditionally made by German monks. That's right: this is a peanut brittle inspired by nuns, made with a beer brewed by monks. How's that for paying homage?

> **COOK'S NOTES** It's important to keep the peanuts warm in the oven as directed before mixing them into the hot melted sugar. This prevents the temperature of the syrup from dropping too abruptly, giving you a bit of extra time to spread the brittle thin before it cools and hardens.
>
> Store the brittle in a sealed container, with a piece of parchment paper between each layer to prevent sticking.

MAKES 4 TO 6 SERVINGS
PREP TIME: 5 MINUTES
COOK TIME: 40 MINUTES

1 cup (150 g) chopped peanuts
5 tablespoons unsalted butter, divided
¼ teaspoon coarse sea salt
¼ teaspoon freshly ground black pepper
1 cup (200 g) sugar
1 tablespoon light corn syrup
½ cup (125 ml) dark beer, preferably a German Doppelbock

Prepare a rimmed sheet pan by lining it with a nonstick silicone baking mat. Alternatively, you can line the sheet pan with parchment paper sprayed with non-stick cooking oil. Set pan aside.

Preheat the oven to 175°F (80°C). Spread the peanuts in a shallow baking dish or pie pan and place them in the warm oven for 5 minutes. Add 1 tablespoon of the butter to the warmed peanuts and stir until it melts, coating the peanuts. Sprinkle peanuts with the salt and pepper, stir to combine and return to the oven to keep warm.

In a large heavy-bottomed saucepan, combine the remaining 4 tablespoons of butter with the sugar, corn syrup and beer. Bring the mixture to a boil over high heat while stirring occasionally. Reduce the heat to medium low, cover and simmer for 5 minutes. Uncover the pot and attach a candy thermometer to the inside. Bring the mixture back to a boil over high heat and continue boiling until the temperature reaches 300°F (150°C). Depending on the heat of your stove, this may take 15 to 20 minutes. Do not stir or shake the pan during this time.

Once the syrup reaches 300°F (150°C), carefully remove the candy thermometer from the pot. Add the warmed peanuts and stir to completely coat with hot syrup. Immediately – and carefully – pour the hot mixture onto the lined sheet pan and spread the brittle into a thin, even layer with a rubber spatula. Work quickly to spread it out before it begins to harden. Allow to cool completely, then break into bite-sized pieces.

UMINOM Along with the toasty, rich malt characteristics that complement the peanuts in this brittle, a German Doppelbock's dark fruit and chocolate notes also harmonize with the brittle's caramelized sugar. If you can't find Doppelbock, other dark beers like porters and stouts will also work well.

GRILLED AND CARAMELIZED BANANA-CUE

In the Philippines, when a word has "cue" on the end, it doesn't always refer to something cooked on a grill. The "cue" suffix actually indicates that the item is served on a stick. For example, *kamote-cue* is sweet potato fried in sugar syrup and served on a skewer, while Liempo-Cue (page 106) is grilled pork belly served on a skewer.

Banana-Cue traditionally denotes bananas fried in a sugar syrup and served on a skewer. For my version of Banana-Cue, I've opted to grill the bananas, because having a wok full of scalding sugar syrup in your kitchen can be problematic.

MAKES 3 TO 6 SERVINGS
PREP TIME: 5 MINUTES
COOK TIME: 5 MINUTES

3 ripe yet firm Saba bananas
¼ cup (65 ml) melted coconut oil
4 tablespoons raw turbinado sugar, or brown sugar

6 bamboo or metal skewers

COOK'S NOTE Saba bananas are easily found at Asian markets. They contain more starch and are thicker than the type commonly found in supermarkets. If you can't find saba bananas, you can use regular bananas – just place them on a skewer whole, rather than cutting them in half.

UMINOM A big, bold imperial stout delivers rich chocolate flavors to complement these sweet caramelized bananas, while also delivering roasted coffee notes that play well with the char and smoke of the grill.

If using bamboo skewers, soak in water for at least 30 minutes prior to grilling. Preheat grill for direct cooking.

Peel the bananas and cut in half lengthwise. Insert a skewer into each banana half and brush all over with coconut oil. Put the sugar on a large plate, then lightly press and roll each banana half in the sugar until well coated.

Place the banana skewers on the grill over direct heat and grill until the sugar caramelizes and melts and grill marks appear on the bananas, 1 to 2 minutes per side. Serve warm.

BEER, CALAMANSI AND COCONUT CREAMSICLES

Think of these sweet frozen treats as a more tropical, beery version of an Orange Creamsicle. Fresh calamansi lime juice, with its bracing tartness and Mandarin orange aroma, is always a great match with rich and creamy coconut milk. And while a run-of-the mill-light industrial lager will do fine in this recipe, a great fruit-forward, juicy IPA can add additional depth with tropical flavors and aromas (think citrus, mango and pineapple). Just be sure to keep these pops away from the kids.

MAKES 10 TO 12 POPSICLES
PREP TIME: 15 MINUTES, PLUS 24 HOURS FOR FREEZING

12 oz (355 ml) pale lager or ale, preferably an India
   pale ale
1 cup (250 ml) coconut milk
½ cup (125 ml) fresh calamansi juice or lime juice
4 tablespoons sugar, plus more to taste

Combine all ingredients in a large pitcher or bowl with a spout and whisk until the sugar is completely dissolved. Taste the mixture and add more sugar if you want it sweeter.

   Pour the mixture into popsicle molds and freeze overnight. Depending on the size of your popsicle molds, you may have extra liquid. If this is the case, just refrigerate the extra liquid in a lidded container, then freeze after the first batch of popsicles have been frozen and removed from the molds.

   To serve, place the popsicle molds under warm running water until the popsicles release.

UMINOM The same beer used to make these popsicles would be a natural pairing for them as well. The beer in your glass will amplify any beer flavors in the popsicles that may have been muted by freezing.

SWEET PURPLE YAM AND COCONUT CHURROS

I was inspired to make these churros after a visit to Disneyland with my oldest son, Bruce. It was May the Fourth – Star Wars Day – and instead of the usual brown cinnamon-sugar churros that are usually sold at the Happiest Place on Earth, they were selling special "Lightsaber" churros covered in red and blue colored sugar. Being a Mace Windu fan, I was sad that they didn't have any purple churros.

So, like a true Jedi, I fashioned my own lightsaber using Filipino purple yam (*ube*) flour and coconut oil. Although these churros aren't purple on the outside, they are vibrantly so on the inside. And it's what's on the inside that counts, right?

MAKES ABOUT 1 DOZEN CHURROS
PREP TIME: 10 MINUTES
COOK TIME: 30 MINUTES

FOR THE CINNAMON SUGAR:
2 teaspoon ground cinnamon
½ cup (100 g) sugar

FOR THE CHURROS:
½ cup (65 g) all-purpose flour
½ cup (95 g) purple yam (ube) flour
1 cup (250 ml) water
½ cup (125 ml) melted coconut oil
1 tablespoon sugar
¼ teaspoon salt
3 eggs, beaten
Canola or peanut oil, for frying

To make the cinnamon sugar, mix together the cinnamon and the ½ cup of sugar on a large rimmed platter. Set aside.

To make the churros, combine the all-purpose flour and the purple yam flour in a small bowl and whisk well to blend. Set aside.

Combine the water, coconut oil, 1 tablespoon sugar and salt in a large saucepan over high heat and bring to a boil. Reduce heat to low, then add the flour mixture all at once. Stir constantly until the mixture forms a ball of dough, about 30 seconds. Remove the pan from the heat, then add the eggs a third at a time into the mixture, stirring after each addition until well incorporated.

Transfer the dough to a large pastry bag fitted with a large star tip. (Alternatively, you can cut a corner from a large zip-top bag and fit a large star tip into the opening.) Set the filled pastry bag in the refrigerator while you heat the frying oil.

Pour oil into a large frying pan or deep skillet to reach a depth of 2 inches (5 cm). Heat the oil over high heat until it reaches 350°F (175°C) on a deep-fry thermometer. Alternatively, you can test the oil by dropping a small bit of dough in; if the dough immediately begins to brown and sizzle, the oil is ready.

When the oil is hot, squeeze lengths of dough from the pastry bag directly into the hot oil to make churros about 4 to 6 inches (10 to 15 cm) long. Working in batches, fry the churros until golden brown, 5 to 10 minutes each. Be sure to adjust the heat as necessary to maintain the oil temperature.

Remove the churros from oil, drain on paper towels, then immediately roll them in the cinnamon-sugar mixture. Serve warm.

UMINOM For these churros, I forgo a chocolate dipping sauce in favor of a robust porter or a decadent stout. With dark malt flavors echoing everything from caramel to coffee to chocolate, these dark beers complement and contrast the coconut aroma, cinnamon spice and sugary sweetness of the churros.

AVOCADO BRULÉE WITH CALAMANSI GRANITA AVOCADO CON HIELO

I have very distinct childhood memories of my maternal grandfather mashing an avocado in a bowl with some crushed ice, a glug of milk, and a heavy sprinkling of sugar (or sweetened condensed milk if we happened to have any in the cupboard). He'd then have at it with a spoon as if he were eating cereal – which was fitting, considering that this avocado and ice mixture probably had as much sugar as the Lucky Charms or Captain Crunch cereal I was so fond of at the time.

   This is my updated version of my Grandfather's avocado and ice – or *avocado con hielo*, as it's known in the Philippines. The avocado gets a crisp shell of bruléed sugar, while the milk and ice are replaced with an easy calamansi granita drizzled with sweetened condensed milk.

MAKES 4 SERVINGS
PREP TIME: 15 MINUTES, PLUS 3 HOURS TO FREEZE THE GRANITA
COOK TIME: 5 MINUTES

FOR THE GRANITA:

3 cups (750 ml) water, divided
1 cup (200 g) sugar
1 teaspoon orange zest
¾ cup (185 ml) fresh calamansi juice or lime juice

FOR THE AVOCADOS:

2 large ripe avocados
2 tablespoons raw sugar

FOR SERVING:

Sweetened condensed milk, for drizzling
Coarse sea salt, to taste

To make the granita, combine ½ cup (125 ml) of the water with the 1 cup of sugar in a medium saucepan over moderately high heat. Add the orange zest, then bring the mixture to a simmer and stir until the sugar dissolves, 2 to 3 minutes. Remove from the heat and pour into a large bowl. Add the remaining 2½ cups (625 ml) water to the bowl, along with the calamansi juice, and stir to combine. Chill the mixture in the refrigerator for at least 1 hour.

   Pour the chilled granita mixture into a shallow baking dish and place in the freezer for 1 hour. After an hour, scrape the frozen areas with a fork, raking the ice crystals toward the center of the dish. Return to the freezer. Continue to freeze, scraping the granita with a fork to break up any large chunks of ice every half hour, until you have fine ice crystals resembling snow. This will take about 3 hours in all.

   When ready to serve, preheat the broiler to high. Cut the avocados in half and remove the pits. Place the sugar on a small plate and press the cut side of the avocados into the sugar to coat. Sprinkle additional sugar on any exposed spots. Place the avocados directly under the broiler with the cut side up and broil for 1 to 2 minutes, or until the sugar has caramelized, melted and formed a crisp crust. Check every 30 seconds or so to make sure the sugar doesn't burn. (Alternatively, you can use a blowtorch for this step.) Remove the avocados from the broiler and allow to cool slightly.

   Carefully scoop the flesh from the avocado skins with a large spoon so that each half remains intact. Place each avocado half in bowl and add a scoop of the granita. Drizzle with sweetened condensed milk and sprinkle with sea salt to serve.

UMINOM With intense bitterness and high levels of alcohol, an imperial IPA has sufficient intensity to contrast both the tartness of the granita and the creamy sweetness of the bruléed avocados.

A Belgian Witbier is a great, lower-alcohol alternative to an imperial IPA. The coriander notes complement the avocado; the citrus flavors match the calamansi; and the high carbonation cuts through the dessert's richness.

ACKNOWLEDGMENTS

Admittedly, writing this cookbook was a lot harder than I thought it would be. Not that I assumed it would be easy – with the experience of writing *The Adobo Road Cookbook* already under my belt, believe me, I knew that writing a second cookbook would be just as difficult a task as the first. The trouble was, I didn't factor in how different my life is now compared to when I wrote *Adobo Road*.

Back then, it was just me, my wife, and our son Bruce, who at that time was a very manageable and not-too-terrible two-year-old. Fast-forward to today: Bruce is seven as I'm writing this, and we've added three-year-old Grant and one-year-old Audrey to the mix. Needless to say, my wife and I have got our hands full. With multiple kids, a fuller work schedule outside of this cookbook and a tighter deadline, my current writing, recipe-testing and food-photography environment was not as stress- or distraction-free as my first go-around.

With all that said, I have to first and foremost thank my wife, Barbara, for helping me stay sane during this entire process, for keeping me calm when the kids weren't (and vice versa) and for just being the best mother, wife and drinking buddy there can be. I guess we've figured out that writing multiple cookbooks is like having multiple kids: We thought we had it figured out after the first one, but man, were we wrong! You da real MVP.

I also want to thank my three kids, Bruce, Grant and Audrey. You three are all the reason I need for anything. I know I always set up my camera and tripod right in the middle of your play area where all your toys are, but that's where the best light in the house is. Thank you for not whacking my camera with your lightsabers, and thank you for not running it over with your baby-doll strollers. The camera will now return to taking pictures of you, rather than of food and beer. I've said it once, and I'll say it again: One day it'll all make sense.

Thank you to my wonderful agent, Vicky Bijur, for seeing my potential, believing in me, and having faith in my work.

Cheers to Chris Cohen for guiding me through the Cicerone exam with the Beer Scholar study guides, and for taking the time to answer my emails when I was stressing about passing the test. I honestly couldn't have done it without you. Thank you!

Many thanks to my editor, Jon Steever, for being understanding and flexible. I need to send you a bottle of Pliny. My gratitude also goes to the rest of the Tuttle Publishing team for giving me yet another opportunity to promote Filipino food and culture through my words, recipes and photos.

And lastly, many thanks to all those out there who continue to support me and my efforts to promote Filipino food and culture. Thank you to everyone who bought a copy of *The Adobo Road Cookbook* and helped to make it a success; because of you, I was fortunate enough to be given another cookbook opportunity. I am forever thankful. *Salamat!*

RESOURCE GUIDE

The Beer Scholar

Website: thebeerscholar.com

The study guides offered at this website are what I relied upon as I prepared for the incredibly difficult Certified Cicerone exam. Without these study guides, I would not have passed the exam. If you're interested in becoming a Certified Cicerone, I highly recommend the Beer Scholar Study Guides.

Cicerone Certification Program

Website: cicerone.org

Provides information, study materials, courses and syllabi to help users prepare for each of the four levels of Cicerone certification.

CraftBeer.com

Website: craftbeer.com

A great resource for information on craft beer and craft beer food pairing.

Eden Canyon Vineyards

Website: edencanyon.com

A Filipino-owned and operated vineyard that makes small-production handcrafted wines in Paso Robles, CA.

Eighth Wonder Rice

Website: heirloomrice.com

Importer and supplier of a number of heirloom rice varieties grown in the Philippines.

FilStop

Website: filstop.com

Online retailer of Filipino ingredients and food products.

Four Winds Growers

Website: fourwindsgrowers.com

Online supplier of potted citrus trees, including calamansi.

Infanta Lambanog

Website: infantalambanog.com

Distiller and supplier of the Philippine coconut wine known as *lambanog*.

Red Boat Fish Sauce

Website: redboatfishsauce.com

Source for premium, award-winning fish sauce made in Vietnam.

Tanduay Rum

Website: tanduayusa.com

Makers of fine Philippine rum distilled from Philippine sugarcane.

ABOUT TUTTLE
"BOOKS TO SPAN THE EAST AND WEST"

Our core mission at Tuttle Publishing is to create books which bring people together one page at a time. Tuttle was founded in 1832 in the small New England town of Rutland, Vermont (USA). Our fundamental values remain as strong today as they were then – to publish best-in-class books informing the English-speaking world about the countries and peoples of Asia. The world has become a smaller place today and Asia's economic, cultural and political influence has expanded, yet the need for meaningful dialogue and information about this diverse region has never been greater. Since 1948, Tuttle has been a leader in publishing books on the cultures, arts, cuisines, languages and literatures of Asia. Our authors and photographers have won numerous awards and Tuttle has published thousands of books on subjects ranging from martial arts to paper crafts. We welcome you to explore the wealth of information available on Asia at **www.tuttlepublishing.com**.

Illustrator Credits: *Shutterstock.com* Incomible 49, 50, 51 (right), 60, 62, 68, 70, 71, 73, 74, 81, 98, 100 (right); Inspiring 53 (right), 84, 95, 104; Mallari 51 (left), 52, 54 (left), 54, 56, 57, 61, 64, 65, 75, 77, 79, 80 (right), 86, 87, 89, 90, 92, 94, 99, 100 (left), 101, 102, 105, 107, 111, 112, 113, 115, 117; Vlad Klok 4, 5, 38, 41

Published by Tuttle Publishing, an imprint of Periplus Editions (HK) Ltd.
www.tuttlepublishing.com
Copyright © 2018 Marvin Gapultos

Library of Congress Cataloging-in-Publication data in process
ISBN: 978-0-8048-4942-5

22 21 20 19 18   5 4 3 2 1

Printed in Hong Kong   1806EP

TUTTLE PUBLISHING® is a registered trademark of Tuttle Publishing, a division of Periplus Editions (HK) Ltd.

DISTRIBUTED BY

North America, Latin America & Europe Tuttle Publishing
364 Innovation Drive
North Clarendon, VT 05759-9436 U.S.A.
Tel: (802) 773-8930   Fax: (802) 773-6993
info@tuttlepublishing.com   www.tuttlepublishing.com

Japan
Tuttle Publishing Yaekari Building, 3rd Floor
5-4-12 Osaki, Shinagawa-ku, Tokyo 141 0032
Tel: (81) 3 5437-0171   Fax: (81) 3 5437-0755
sales@tuttle.co.jp   www.tuttle.co.jp

Asia Pacific
Berkeley Books Pte. Ltd.
61 Tai Seng Avenue #02-12, Singapore 534167
Tel: (65) 6280-1330   Fax: (65) 6280-6290
inquiries@periplus.com.sg   www.periplus.com